UNITED IRISHMAN

The Autobiography of James Hope

Edited and Introduced by

John Newsinger

MERLIN PRESS

First published in 2001
by the Merlin Press Ltd.
P.O. BOX 30705
LONDON
WC2E 8QD

© John Newsinger 2001

*British Library Cataloguing in Publication Data
is available from the British Library*

ISBN: 0850364965

Typeset by: Bruce Brine

Printed in the UK

'the most remarkable events in which I was a humble actor'

—James Hope

FOR LORNA

Contents

Acknowledgements

Thanks to friends and colleagues at Bath Spa University College, especially to Brian Griffin and Graham Davis, Irish Studies stalwarts. Thanks are due as well to a former colleague, Margaret Ward. Thanks to Alan Marshall for his help and encouragement. Special thanks to my typists: Margaret Tremeer and Carol Slade. And, of course, to my family. Also to Tony Zurbrugg for his patience. Lastly, to the Inter-Library Loans Service at Bath Spa University College who are without doubt the best.

Introduction:

James Hope, the United Irishmen and 1798

The United Irish movement and the 1798 Rebellion briefly opened a window of opportunity in Ireland, a window which in Kevin Whelan's words 'beckoned to the still unattained prospect of a non-sectarian, democratic and inclusive politics adequately representing the Irish people in all their inherited complexities'.[1] A republican union of all Irishmen threatened to bring down the Protestant Ascendancy, to overthrow aristocratic rule and end the colonial connection with Britain. The window was forcibly closed by the British, making use of a combination of violence and sectarianism, that allowed them to divide and conquer. Even so, the defeat and destruction of the United Irishmen was by no means certain. In the words of Lord Castlereagh, one of the architects of the movement's defeat, 'there never was in any country so formidable an effort on the part of the people'.[2] The outcome of the conflict was arguably still in the balance as late as the end of May to the beginning of June 1798. Among the participants in these events was James Hope, a working-class Ulster Protestant, a weaver by trade, born at Templepatrick in County Antrim in August 1765.

Hope joined the United Irish movement in 1795 and became one of its most successful emissaries, travelling through Ulster and Leinster, organizing and recruiting both Catholics and Protestants. When the time finally came to take up arms in June 1798, he was one of those who insisted, despite the leadership's opposition, that the North had to rise. He played his part in the unsuccessful United Irish attack on Antrim town, acting as a lieutenant to Henry Joy McCracken. In the aftermath of defeat, Hope avoided arrest, remaining at large to participate in Robert Emmet's abortive 1803 Rising. Once again he escaped arrest, surviving the final collapse of the movement, and triumph of the British.

Forty years later, he was to recall these events in a memoir that he prepared for Richard R. Madden, the historian of the United Irishmen. That memoir appeared in Madden's *Antrim and Down in '98*, published in Glasgow. Why republish it today? First of all, any United Irish memoir is of interest as an account of a revolutionary movement that aspired to unite Protestant and Catholic and that proved popular and powerful enough to mount a serious challenge to British rule in Ireland.

Hope is of particular interest, however, because he was a working-class Protestant participant whose account provides a particularly distinctive view of the movement. While the United Irish movement can be best regarded as an attempt to carry out a bourgeois revolution in Ireland, replicating the American and French Revolutions, Hope provides a working-class critique of the enterprise. He exposes the class differences and the class contradictions that were an inevitable part of such a movement. It is a mistake to regard him, as A. T. Q. Stewart does, as 'a very remarkable man, a pioneer socialist before socialism had been articulated as a political creed'.[3] Certainly he was a remarkable man, in the words of one fellow revolutionary, 'a man whose talents were far above his fortunes',[4] but his ideas and attitudes can be better regarded as a species of plebeian radicalism that displayed a clear understanding of class antagonism and class conflict, but not, as yet, an identification with socialism as the way forward. This way of thinking was arguably a feature of the left-wing of all the revolutionary movements of the 1780s and 1790s. Hope himself makes absolutely clear his distrust of the middle-class elements within the movement and his belief that it was this that in good part accounted for his success at avoiding arrest. Certainly, his part in the events of these years, his class consciousness and his Protestantism make his memoir of the United Irish movement of exceptional interest.

Before proceeding to Hope's memoir, however, some preliminary account of these tumultuous years is necessary.

The United Irishmen

The United Irish movement had its origins in the increasing social weight of the middle class, both Catholic and Protestant, in Irish society in the last decades of the eighteenth century. Economic advance had produced a growing middle class (merchants and traders, businessmen and industrialists, large farmers and lawyers) in both town and country who, despite their increasing wealth, found themselves excluded from political influence by an aristocratic elite that maintained itself in power as a Protestant Ascendancy. The Protestant middle class, both North and South, inspired by the American Revolution, had placed considerable hope for the remedy of its grievances in the Volunteer movement and Grattan's Parliament in the early 1780s. The achievements of these years proved more apparent than real with the Irish government remaining in the hands of a corrupt aristocracy allied with the British.

What made this situation intolerable was the great French Revolution of 1789. As far as middle-class Protestants were concerned the overthrow of the French monarchy and the French nobility provided ample demonstration that history was on their side and that the old order was doomed throughout Europe. Moreover, it also showed that a Catholic people could carry out a revolution, that the Catholics were, in France at least, in the vanguard of the struggle for Liberty. This had important implications for Ireland, opening up for many middle-class Protestants the prospect of an alliance with the Catholic middle class against their common enemies. A key figure in the realization of these possibilities was Theobald Wolfe Tone, author in 1791 of *An Argument on Behalf of the Catholics of Ireland*, a powerful and influential call for Protestant–Catholic unity.

Tone, a Dublin lawyer, was involved in the establishment of the Society of United Irishmen in Belfast in October 1791. Its founders were all prominent Presbyterian businessmen, among them Samuel McTier, Samuel Neilson, William Sinclair, Thomas McCabe, Henry Haslett, William Tennant, John Campbell, and William and Robert Simms. They committed themselves to parliamentary reform as the way to bring the government under middle-class control and to a union with the Catholic middle class to achieve it.[5]

Soon after, in November 1791, a sister society was established in Dublin. Once again, this was a resolutely bourgeois body with a solid middle-class membership, both Catholics and Protestants. According to one study, the membership 'was composed of professional and business men with a sprinkling of country gentlemen ... The businessmen included over 100 merchants (of whom 67 were cloth merchants), 31 textile manufacturers, an iron founder (who claimed to have installed the first steam engine in Dublin), a pin-maker, tailors, jewellers, hatters, hosiers and butchers'. There was also a large contingent of lawyers.[6] The Irish equivalent of the French Third Estate was beginning to ready itself for the struggle for power.

The ambitions of the Protestant middle class were in many ways shared by their Catholic fellows. The eighteenth century, despite the penal laws, had seen the emergence of a class of prosperous Catholic businessmen and professionals.[7] They were determined to achieve both a larger voice in the affairs of the Catholic community and a stake in the government of the country. Many of them became United Irishmen. In December

1791, they captured control of the Catholic Committee, over-throwing its aristocratic-clerical leadership (Lord Fingall was physically removed from the chair) and launched an aggressive campaign for Catholic Emancipation. The ubiquitous Tone became secretary to the committee. This campaign, arguably as important as Daniel O'Connell's 1820s campaign, has been neglected by historians. It culminated in the election of a Catholic Convention, very much modelled on the French experi-ence, and succeeded in extracting significant concessions from the British government in the face of fierce opposition from the Protestant Ascendancy.[8] In early 1793, the Catholic Relief Act was carried through the Irish Parliament granting Catholics the right to vote (although there was no democratization of the franchise), but not the right to stand for election. This victory was the high-water mark of the constitutional movement.

In its first phase the Society of United Irishmen saw itself as a propagandist organization, campaigning for parliamentary reform and advocating a union of all Irishmen, celebrating the French Revolution and expressing solidarity with radicals in England and Scotland. A vital instrument in the organization's propaganda activities was the *Northern Star* newspaper that first appeared in Belfast on 4 January 1792. Twelve members of the Belfast Society put up £2,000 and under the editorship of Samuel Neilson, 'the driving force behind the paper', threw down a powerful challenge to the Protestant Ascendancy.[9] Appearing twice weekly, the paper reached a circulation of over 4,000, although it was actually read by or to considerably more people. Neilson himself claimed that every copy was on average read by ten people. Men were actually employed to read the newspaper to others.

The *Northern Star* expressed considerable sympathy for the ideas of Tom Paine, favourably reviewing his writings, published extracts from William Godwin's *Enquiry Concerning Political Justice* and carried notices advertising Mary Wollstonecraft's *A Vindication of the Rights of Women*. It gave considerable attention to events in France, but also took up other causes, for example, condemning the slave trade and opposing repression in England and Scotland. Probably most effective were the satirical assaults that the paper mounted: 'Trial of Hurdy Gurdy', 'Billy Bluff and the Squire' and 'The Lion of Old England', all reprinted as pamphlets with a large circulation. The paper published its own 'Political Dictionary', providing useful definitions:

ARISTOCRATS: Tyrants who arrogate to themselves privileges, by which they engross the wealth of the country, and keep the people in subjection by force or corruption.

FREEDOM: An obsolete word, at present supplied by the word SLAVERY.[10]

Certainly, the newspaper's success seriously alarmed the government and its supporters. One loyalist, John Schoales complained that the 'infernal paper' was 'the principal and most powerful of all the instruments used for agitating and deluding the minds of the people ... The lowest of the people get it. It is read to them in clusters. A whole neighbourhood subscribe to it'.[11]

As far as the United Irish leadership was concerned in this phase of the movement's development, the society's purpose was to educate Protestant and Catholic opinion, while relying on the agency of the Volunteers to play the same role they had played in 1782, extracting concessions from the British government by threats and intimidation rather than by violence. This was not to be. With the outbreak of war between Britain and France in February 1793 the British government became increasingly determined to support the Protestant Ascendancy in Ireland, endorsing whatever means were thought necessary to sustain it. The Irish government resorted to repression in an effort to silence the United Irishmen, eliminate the Volunteer threat and cow the Catholics. This policy provoked the radicalization of the United Irishmen, its transformation into a mass underground revolutionary army organized for armed insurrection.

According to William Drennan, a Dublin United Irishman, the government's intention was 'to get rid of us by prosecution, persecution, or the terror of it'.[12] The government's measures had some success, at least initially, harassing the movement's leaders, scaring off the moderates (among them Drennan!) and effectively closing the door on constitutional agitation. One effect of this repression was to decisively shift the movement's centre of gravity. With the moderates withdrawing, more radical elements came to the fore, elements that were prepared to embrace an alliance with the lower classes. It was not so much that men like Tone, Neilson or John and Henry Sheares were radicalized by repression as that repression created the context for their radicalism to carry the day.[13] Indeed, one account of this transitional moment in the United Irishmen's history very much sees the initiative as coming from below. Marianne Elliott argues that in 1794 the society in Belfast was moribund, except for one branch

that had happened to escape official vigilance because of 'the obscurity of its members'. It was this branch and another political club quite separate from the United Irishmen and said to be composed of 'mechanics, petty shopkeepers and farmers' who were the first to join together as an oath-bound republican organization. They retained the name of the United Irishmen.

She insists that this 'was not simply a continuation of the original Society' and that 'for some time the main United leaders remained unaware of its development'.[14] The implications of this are clear: the initiative for revolutionary organization in Ireland came from below, from that same social group that constituted the *sansculottes* of the French Revolution. The middle-class leaders, or at least the most determined and the most radical of them, threw in their lot with the plebeian classes, with the artisans, the workers, the shopkeepers and the tenant farmers.

The Revolutionary Turn

The appointment of the Whig politician Lord Fitzwilliam as Viceroy in January 1795 seemed to promise an end to repression and the possibility of further instalments of reform. His recall the following month was taken as representing the triumph of the Protestant Ascendancy. He was replaced by Lord Camden, a man prepared to wholeheartedly endorse the policies of the Ascendancy hardliners.

The Fitzwilliam affair strengthened the hand of those determined to reorganize the United Irishmen as a revolutionary underground uniting both Catholics and Protestants. In Ulster, the open clubs were replaced with a cell structure. Cells with thirty-five members were formed, with three cells forming a company and ten companies forming a regiment. Regiments were commanded by a colonel and at county level the various colonels elected a commanding officer, the adjutant general. On 10th May 1795 the new organizational structure, together with a new constitution, were formally adopted by representatives of seventy-two United Irish societies. The system spread rapidly throughout Ulster, incorporating Volunteer companies and Defender societies. County organizations were established in Antrim and Down and in August 1795 an Ulster Directory was formed.[15] Among those who joined the movement in the summer of 1795 was James Hope.

A vital factor in the United movement's growth in the North (and later elsewhere) was its alliance with the Defender secret societies. Defenderism had its origins in County Armagh in the 1780s as a Catholic response to the activities of the Protestant Peep O'Day boys. By the early 1790s, the movement had spread beyond Armagh and was regarded by the Dublin government as a serious threat. While its origins were sectarian, in fact the Defenders saw Protestant loyalists as their enemies rather than Protestants as such. Indeed, by the mid-1790s, in some areas Protestants were actually joining the movement. It had started out as a movement committed to the defence of Catholic tenant formers and artisans against the Protestant Ascendancy and its agents, but increasingly came to adopt a revolutionary posture, looking to the French example and allying itself, indeed eventually merging with, the United Irishmen.[16] According to James Hope, United Irishmen and Defenders became 'sworn brothers'. This was the result of a 'plan of union projected by Neilson, assisted by Luke Teeling of Lisburn ... a linen merchant of the first rank and a Roman Catholic'.[17] Hope himself was to play a role as liaison between the United Irish leadership and the Defenders. This alliance was very much a necessary response to the repression that descended on both movements.

The Ulster Directory was determined to spread its system of underground organization to Dublin. Here it was resisted by the moderate United Irish leaders, but found favour in the plebeian clubs that had developed as part of the popular response to the French Revolution. Defenderism was a significant force in the city by the summer of 1795 with some 4,000 sworn members, the great majority Catholics, but including some Protestants. The Defenders overlapped with the radical clubs of the metropolis of which the best known is the Philanthropic. The leading figure in the Philanthropic was John Burke, a former Trinity College student, expelled for atheism and involved in various stillborn plans for the seizure of Dublin Castle and the arming of the people.[18] In the summer of 1796 the Ulster Directory sent James Hope and James Metcalfe as emissaries to Dublin to establish contact with the city's political underground. Hope had, in his own words, been charged 'to disseminate our views among the working classes.[19] The intention was to persuade the Dublin radicals to establish a disciplined United Irish organization along the same lines as in Ulster with a revolutionary leadership directing the struggle. As James Smyth argues, Hope's claims of success in this endeavour are confirmed by other sources.[20]

The Dublin government responded to the spread of Defenderism and the growing United Irish threat with intensifying repression. In 1795 Lord Carhampton, the Commander-in-Chief, 'dragooned' Connacht, burning houses and torturing suspects, in an attempt to root out the Defenders. Hundreds of men were arrested and despatched to the Royal Navy as impressed seamen. This was a foretaste of what Ulster was to suffer two years later. Early in 1796 an Indemnity Act and Insurrection Act were rushed through the Irish Parliament, draconian measures that even alarmed the British government in London. The one indemnified magistrates against any illegal acts they might commit (for example, torture) and the other introduced a battery of repressive measures that included the death penalty for administering illegal oaths and transportation for taking one. Later that year, the government suspended *habeas corpus* and began what was in effect the internment of United Irish leaders. In September Samuel Neilson, Thomas Russell, eighteen-year-old Charles Teeling and others were arrested in Belfast and carried off to prison in Dublin. Large crowds cheered them on their way. Even these measures failed to contain the situation, let along turn the tide.

How close the British were to losing Ireland only became apparent at the end of 1796 when a French fleet of forty-eight ships, carrying some 20,000 veteran troops commanded by one of the Revolution's best generals, Lazare Hoche, set sail for Bantry Bay. The expedition was accompanied by Wolfe Tone, the principal architect of the United Irish alliance with the French. They were to land, raise the standard of revolt, seize Cork, march on Dublin and proclaim an Irish Republic. Tone had assured the French that the country would rise in their support. Unfortunately, the plan misfired. Hoche was separated from the rest of the fleet (Hope suspected treachery!) which arrived off the Cork coast, waited in vain for their commander-in-chief, before being dispersed by storms. A marvellous opportunity to strike a decisive blow against the British Empire had miscarried.[21] As Tone himself observed in his journal, 'England has not had such an escape since the Spanish Armada, and that expedition like ours, was defeated by the weather; the elements fight against us, and courage is here of no avail'.[22]

The seriousness of the situation as made absolutely clear by the leading hardliner in the Dublin government, John Beresford:

We had two days after they were at anchor in Bantry Bay, from Cork to Bantry less than 3,000 men, two pieces of artillery, and no magazine of any kind ... No landing was made. Providence prevented it; if there had, where was a stand to be made? It is clear that Cork was gone; who would answer afterwards for the loyalty of the country then in possession of the French? Would the northern parts of the country have remained quiet? Not an hour.[23]

Despite the threat at Bantry Bay, the government had to keep large numbers of troops in Ulster for fear of a rising. The Chief Secretary, Lord Pelham actually ordered the immediate suppression of the *Northern Star* in the event of French troops landing. If a landing had taken place, it seems certain that a rising would have followed regardless. The British would have been driven out of the country and an Irish Republic established in Dublin. This was not to be.

The attempt, even though it failed, had two important consequences for Ireland. First, it gave a tremendous boost to the United Irish movement. While this first expedition had failed, the United Irish leaders promised that a further attempt would certainly be made and that allied with a French army their victory was assured. Thousands rallied to their cause. The second consequence was that the British and Irish governments realized the danger they were in and determined to crush the United Irishmen by whatever means were necessary.

Bourgeois Revolution and Social Radicalism in Ireland

According to Sir Richard Musgrave, the hardline Unionist historian of the 1798 Rebellion, an important cause of the involvement of Northern Protestants in the United Irish movement was simply the 'jealousy of the linen drapers, who made immense fortunes, towards the nobility and gentry, seized of old hereditary estates, on account of their superior weight and respectability'. Further on, he asserts that: 'Some linen-drapers, from motives of envy which I have already stated, encouraged their workmen in imbibing the new revolutionary doctrines'.[24] Musgrave successfully identified the mainspring of the whole affair, although he never developed the point, being more concerned with revealing the 1798 Rebellion to have been a Catholic plot to extirpate Protestantism. But what does his momentary insight tell us about the character of the Irish Rebellion, coming on as it did in the wake of the American and

French Revolutions and forming part of the so-called Atlantic Revolution of the closing decades of the eighteenth and opening decades of the nineteenth centuries?

For most contemporary historians the Irish Rebellion was a product of modernization, whether it be the work of modernizing elites or a product of the strains of modernization. In fact, the Rebellion can best be seen as an attempted bourgeois revolution, a bourgeois revolution that was defeated and failed. The Irish middle class, Protestant and Catholic, with a leadership dominated by manufacturers and merchants, engaged in an attempt to overthrow the power of the great landowners, an attempt that necessitated breaking the connection with Britain whose support sustained those landowners in power. They intended to remake Irish society in their own image. Indeed, the composition of the United Irish leadership positively lends itself to this Marxist interpretation with even more transparency than do the American and French Revolutions. As Nancy Curtin has pointed out:

> The social composition of the United Irish activists displayed a strong bias toward trade, commerce and industry, although the range in social status may have been very wide indeed. Class antagonisms were no doubt a potent factor in the origin and development of the United Irish movement. But one of the clearest manifestations of these antagonisms was the conflict between a rising and self-conscious middle-class power and a hereditary landed class with a monopoly of political power ... It was this commercial, industrial and professional class that shaped the ideology and aims of the United Irishmen.[25]

Clearly, the project these men were engaged in was a classic bourgeois revolution. They intended to overthrow the great landowners, and although such an endeavour would require popular support, the world they hoped to create would be a world founded on their particular class interests.

How else to explain the revolutionary politics and commitment to armed insurrection of businessmen, manufacturers and merchants? Henry Joy McCracken, for example, came from a successful business background. His grandfather had founded the *Belfast Newsletter* and had owned a major paper-making company. He, together with his brothers and sisters, was involved in the textile industry. At the age of twenty-two, he was managing a cotton mill. Samuel Neilson had his own textile business and used his wealth to finance the *Northern*

Star. Oliver Bond was another substantial textile merchant. Henry Jackson, Bond's father-in-law, was a substantial industrialist, owning factories in Dublin, including an iron foundry, where large numbers of pikes were made for the United Irish cause. His foreman/clerk, Edward Dunn was one of Hope's contacts in Dublin and his workers were United Irish to a man. Jackson even called his country house 'Fort Paine'. The bourgeois credentials of the United Irish leadership are securely established.

What of their political programme? If there had been a successful Irish revolution in 1797 or 1798 there can be little doubt that historians would regard Arthur O'Connor's pamphlet, *The State of Ireland* as its seminal document. It was the Irish equivalent of Sieyés *What Is The Third Estate?* which, according to James Livesey, actually provided O'Connor with his model. Of course, O'Connor was not a businessman or merchant, but a country gentleman, who had embraced the teachings of Adam Smith (on one occasion he was described as bad company because of his tendency to talk 'a few pages of Adam Smith in lieu of conversation') and had, moreover, drawn revolutionary conclusions from them. He had become a fervent supporter of the French Revolution after a visit to France in 1792, emerged as one of the leaders of the United Irishmen after his return home, and was the moving force behind the Dublin revolutionary newspaper, the *Press.* His *The State of Ireland* was published in 1798. It mounted a staunch defence of the French Revolution, blaming counter-revolution and foreign intervention, in particular Britain, for the consequent bloodshed, suffering and war. It condemned the British Empire in absolutely uncompromising terms. And, it proclaimed that 'Industry is the source of human prosperity', whether it be agriculture, commerce, fisheries or manufacturing. In Ireland, however, the country's wealth, its capital, has been squandered for the benefit of Britain with the connivance of the Irish Parliament. He asked,

> Does the produce of the lands of Ireland go to supply the fund for the employment of its People? No! your corn, your cattle, your butter, your leather, your yarn, all your superfluous produce, and much more that would be superfluous if the People of Ireland were furnished with the common necessaries of life are all exported without a return to pay the rents of Irish Landlords who do not think the country worthy of their residence, every particle

of which is as utterly lost to the fund for the employment of the People of Ireland as if it had been thrown into the sea.

And as for trade and industry: the Legislator has thrown open every market in Ireland to every species of British manufacture, whilst every market in Britain is shut against every species of Irish manufacture, with one solitary exception, which, after every effort, British industry could not compass. Your Legislature has not only sacrificed your home trade to the most commercial nation in the world, but, by giving this powerful nation an unbounded right to fill your markets with the produce of her own and every other nation, while a reciprocal right of sending foreign produce to her markets is strictly denied you, your foreign trade undergoes the fate of your home trade.

The Irish Parliament, he insisted, acts not in the interests of Ireland but in the interests of Britain. The Irish government are just so many 'prostitute hirelings' who have committed 'the foulest treason against the people of Ireland'. The solutions were 'CATHOLIC EMANCIPATION', 'POPULAR REPRESENTATION' and 'NATIONAL LIBERTY'. Revolution was, he urged, nothing to be afraid of. The Irish people, he concluded, 'will put down your oppressors without disgracing yourselves; and you will set up the liberties of your country in a manner that will cover you with glory...'.[26]

For many of the United Irish leaders, the world they hoped to create did not include trade unions. This has surprised some historians, who have seen it as indicating a conservatism on their part, as calling into question their revolutionary credentials.[27] It is, in fact, exactly what one would expect from bourgeois revolutionaries. When in 1792 Samuel Neilson and the *Northern Star* called for the suppression of Belfast's embryonic trade union movement, he was pursuing his class interests, the same class interests that led him into a revolutionary confrontation with the British and Irish governments. Similarly, that same year, when Thomas Dry, another United Irish leader, prosecuted workers for trade union activity in Dublin, he was following his class interests.[28]

This is not the whole story, however. As it became clear that the movement's objectives could only be realized by revolution and that this would only be possible with mass popular support, so a section of the United Irish leadership began to espouse a more radical, egalitarian politics. This was partly from genuine sympathy with the poor and partly from political necessity. At this point, some of the more moderate elements began to withdraw from the movement, helped on their way by government repression. Others pinned their hopes on French intervention, which would avoid the need for a revolutionary outbreak, or at least make it easier to control, but a section of the leadership was radicalized. This was all part of the revolutionary process.

In an important article that appeared in the journal *Irish Historical Studies* in November 1998, James Quinn took issue with the view of the United Irish leadership as conservative on social issues, arguing that it was too one-sided. He insisted that there had always been an 'egalitarian strain in their thinking' and that this had become more pronounced 'after 1794 when they began to form themselves into a popular revolutionary movement'. As the movement developed a popular mass base, so it 'incorporated elements that were not prepared to await the progressive legislation of a reformed parliament, and various schemes to alleviate the plight of the poor, often involving immediate social upheaval, were circulated on local initiative'. While many of the leaders remained unsympathetic to this radicalism, others, in particular, Henry Joy McCracken, Thomas Russell and, by the later 1790s, Samuel Neilson, were to embrace it.[29]

Thomas Russell, a former British army officer, who had fought in India, provides an interesting case study of a middle class republican wrestling with social radicalism. In his diary he writes of talking politics with a Protestant mill worker in February 1793. They are drinking whiskey in the man's cabin:

> Says, 'I think liberty worth risquing life for. In a cause of that sort I think I should have courage enough from reflection to brave death'. One of his children was climbing on his knee. 'As for my part,' says he, 'it does not much signify now as to myself but it grieves me to breed up these children to be slaves. I would gladly risque all to prevent that.' When will a man of fortune in Ireland reason thus? Our senators and great think of nothing but their own sordid interests. Here was a peasant interested for the freedom of mankind. Such I have frequently met.

He goes on in the same entry to observe that 'Power and wealth corrupt and harden the heart', concluding that 'Property must be alter'd in some measure'. In a later entry, in July, he notes a fellow United Irishman insisting 'that it's the lower orders alone who will produce a revolution. When the majority feel themselves slaves they will resist'. Russell goes on to conclude that

> From all I can see, the men of property all through Ireland, whether landed or commercial, are decidedly against a struggle ... The people are beginning to see this and in time when they feel their strength and injurys will do it themselves and then adieu to property.

Of course, this is not to argue that Russell was some sort of premature socialist. Rather, he recognized that it was the lower classes who would be the mainstay of any revolutionary attempt and that their plebeian radicalism would not be content with parliamentary reform and national independence. There would not be any abolition of private property, but the overthrow of the rich would very likely be accompanied by a redistribution of their property. In December 1793 he recorded another conversation to the effect that eventually the people will 'take the matter in their own hands and then woe to their oppressors and the rich. The example of France will be followed and perhaps exceeded'.[30]

Where does James Hope fit into this? He was, in many ways, the arch exponent of plebeian radicalism, a radicalism that, in his case, derived from his experience of life as a weaver. He complained that the gap between the classes in Ireland was so wide 'that mankind seemed divided into different species'. The conclusion he drew from this was that 'the condition of the labouring class was the fundamental question at issue between the rulers and the ruled, and there could be no solid foundation for liberty till measures were adopted that went to the root of the evil'. For too many in the United Irish leadership the struggle 'was merely between commercial and aristocratical interests, to determine which should have the people as its prey, each contending for the greatest share'. As far as he was concerned, 'so long as men of rank and fortune lead the people, they will modify abuses, reform to a certain extent, but they never will remove any real grievances that press down the people'. The manner in which the United Irish movement went down to defeat in 1798 only confirmed his opinion.[31]

One last point worth making about the United Irish movement is its internationalism. This concerned not just the inspiration it drew from the American and French revolutions, but also its determined attempts to establish a revolutionary alliance with the radical movements in Scotland and England. Indeed, according to Marianne Elliott an awareness of United Irish activities in England is 'fundamental to a proper understanding of their aims and development, particularly after 1797'.[32] They established links with and encouraged the most radical elements in Scotland and England, helping to set up the shadowy United Englishmen and United Scotsmen organizations.[33] Elliott goes on to make a vital point with regard to this dimension of United Irish activity:

> The United Irishmen's campaign was not a republican struggle in the narrow nationalist sense of their twentieth century successors. Even its lower ranks saw the English people as friends and in 1797 reports from the leaders of successful missionizing in England and Scotland proved as potent a boost to morale as promises of French help.[34]

The Road to Rebellion

In the aftermath of Bantry Bay, United Irish membership in the province of Ulster increased dramatically, according to one account, doubling between January and April 1797. The movement was particularly strong in counties Antrim and Down. Whereas in July 1795 the two counties had a membership of some 5,000, by May 1797 the number had risen to 48,000. By the middle of 1797 United Irish membership throughout the whole of Ulster (all nine counties) was approaching 120,000.[35] While attention has usually focused on Antrim and Down, the two counties that 'turned out' in 1798, it will not do to underestimate the extent of the organization elsewhere. A study of the movement's strength and influence in County Tyrone, for example, argues that by the early summer of 1797 they had achieved an ascendancy in the county and were in a position to seize power.[36] Outside of Ulster, the organization remained weak with the Leinster counties (including Dublin) only accounting for some 16,000 men. This was to change towards the end of 1797 and into early 1798 when the movement's centre of gravity began to shift towards Dublin.

Kevin Whelan has provided a marvellous account of the United Irish movement's propaganda activities, activities that amounted to a successful attempt to politicize popular culture. He characterizes this (drawing on the work of the Italian Marxist, Antonio Gramsci) as a 'war of position'. The movement's propaganda 'skilfully blended international, national and local issues, addressing long-nurtured feelings of exclusion and historical injustice'. The radical press, a host of pamphlets and ballads, the network of plebeian clubs and societies and a repertoire of defiant communal activities gave the movement the necessary vigour and vitality to survive intensifying repression. The Irish and British governments were confronted by a popular revolutionary movement that was almost daily growing in strength and influence. Whelan is surely correct when he argues that the revolutionaries had 'easily won the propaganda war'. Even when driven underground, the movement continued to hold clandestine meetings:

> Under the aegis of sporting meetings and communal festivities—cock-fights, wrestling matches, horse-races, patterns, dinner parties, pilgrimages, bonfires, wakes, turf-cuttings, dances, balls, spinning beer, confraternities. The informer Thomas Boyle described a typical example— a cock-fight in a barn at Clonard on the Meath/Kildare border, attended by one hundred men, ninety of whom took the United Irish oath ... Public displays were also used by the United Irishmen to make explicit the power of numbers: political funerals, potato-diggings, harvestings and turf-cuttings were not simply solidarity demonstrations, but a celebration of the local strength of adherence to the cause and a calculated, intimidating gesture of defiance.[37]

But having lost the propaganda war, the government resorted to more direct, more brutal, methods.

While the French arrival at Bantry Bay gave considerable encouragement to the United Irishmen, it also caused considerable alarm in official circles. The seriousness of the revolutionary threat was at last realized. The Irish government took the decision to crush the revolutionary movement in Ulster before the French could return. General Gerard Lake was ordered to use whatever methods were necessary to pacify the province, to stamp out the state of 'smothered rebellion', that existed there.[38]

The methods employed by Lake were extremely brutal, including widespread use of torture, the looting and burning of houses and even murder. One of the worst episodes involved a Welsh cavalry unit, the 'Ancient Britons' searching for arms around Newry. A militia officer, John Gifford complained that he was able to find them 'by the smoke and flames of burning houses and by the dead bodies of boys and men slain by the

Britons, though no opposition whatever had been given by them ... From ten to twenty were killed outright; many wounded, and eight houses burned'.[39] Suspects were routinely flogged, picketed (stretched on the ground) or half-hanged in order to extract confessions and discover arms caches. These methods were to be joined by 'pitch-capping' (coating the head with pitch which was then set on fire). As Lake put it in a letter to the Chief Secretary, Lord Pelham in May 1797: 'these villains do most undoubtedly mediate a rising and that very shortly ... Nothing but terror will keep them in order'. Pelham was nevertheless still able, in the traditional British manner, to reassure himself that 'so strong a measure could not have been carried into execution with more temper, mildness and firmness.[40]

This punitive campaign, the so-called 'dragooning' of Ulster, was not enough on its own though. The province remained discontented and rebellious. In the circumstances, the government decided to exploit the sectarian conflict that had broken out in County Armagh and had prompted the establishment of the Orange Order in the autumn of 1795.[41] This organization became the embodiment of hardline Protestantism, committed to keeping the Catholics down by brute force. While initially, the Orange Order was seen as yet another threat to public order, the United Irish menace soon led to it being regarded as an unsavoury but nevertheless vital ally. It offered the prospect of undermining the Protestant-Catholic unity that the United Irishmen were painstakingly seeking to establish and of enlisting hitherto disaffected Protestants on the side of the government.

The key figure here was General John Knox, himself an Ulster landowner, based at Dungannon, and like Lake a staunch advocate of terror. On 18 March 1797 he wrote to Lake admitting that the main purpose of his military operations was not to disarm the population but 'to increase the animosity between the Orangemen and United Irishmen ... Upon that animosity depends the safety of the centre counties of the North'. Without the Orangemen, he went on, 'the whole of Ulster would be as bad as Antrim and Down'. He urged Pelham to allow him to incorporate the Orangemen into the yeomanry. They were, he insisted, 'the only description of men in the North or Ireland that can be depended upon'. He admitted they were 'bigots', but they were 'the only barrier we have against the United Irishmen'. If only he could be allowed to 'encourage the Orangemen ... I shall be able to put down the United Irishmen in Armagh, Monaghan, Cavan and part of Tyrone'.[42] The general's brother, Thomas Knox, an Irish Member of Parliament, was if anything, even more explicit: 'As to the Orangemen, we have rather a difficult card to play. They must not be entirely discountenanced; on the contrary we must in a certain degree uphold them for, with all their licentiousness, on them must we rely for the preservation of our lives and properties should critical times occur'.[43] Pelham left the decision up to the men on the spot.

Confronted with the threat of revolution, the British and Irish governments played the 'Orange card'. They resorted to the deliberate encouragement of sectarian conflict, encouraging and arming the Orange Order, incorporating its members into the Crown forces. This point requires emphasizing because so many historians find it difficulty to accept that this was the case. Indeed, some accounts actually blame the rise of Protestant sectarianism not on the governments that encouraged it, but on the United Irishmen who did their best to unite Protestant and Catholic in the struggle for national independence.[44] This is just perverse: those who oppose sectarianism encourage it by opposing it! Whereas the United Irishmen sent emissaries into Armagh in an attempt to calm the situation and establish a truce between the warring parties, the government determined to exacerbate the conflict. One Armagh magistrate, the Reverend Charles Warburton, despite some suspicion of the Orangemen, actually concluded that 'the enemies of our establishment have reduced us to make "divide" a justifiable measure'.[45] In Kevin Whelan's words, the attempt by the revolutionaries to 'create united Irishmen was rebuffed by a deliberate effort to create disunited Irishmen'.[46]

Another area where the United Irishmen suffered a serious setback was with regard to their attempts to penetrate and subvert the militia and yeomanry forces that the Irish government had raised locally. Many United Irishmen joined these military units with the intention of winning their fellow soldiers over to the revolutionary cause. They had considerable success in this, but the failure of the rebellion to take place in 1797 (a point we shall return to) gave the authorities enough time to root out the subversive threat in their own ranks. British success in this endeavour was an important factor in their defeat of the 1798 Rebellion. This did not stop James Hope masquerading as a militia sergeant while touring the country.

The army camp at Blaris, near Lisburn, was regarded as a United Irish stronghold with perhaps as many as 1,600 men sworn into the movement. One Dublin Castle official wrote that the 'whole camp is at the disposal of Belfast, but they intend to keep still until the harvest is in'.[47] They kept still too long. In May 1797 the United Irish network in the Monaghan Militia, based in the camp, was uncovered and four 'ringleaders' were identified and arrested: Daniel Gillan, Peter Carron and the brothers Owen and William McKenna. Instead of carrying out a wholesale purge of the disaffected, which, because of the numbers involved, might well have provoked a serious mutiny, it was decided to make an example of these four. On 17 May, they were shot, kneeling on their coffins in front of their comrades. The failure to prevent these executions was a decisive moment.[48] While many individual militiamen remained loyal to the revolutionary cause, the majority were successfully intimidated. They renewed their allegiance to the Crown and were to play an important part in the defeat of the United Irish cause.

The consequences of the failure to save the four from the firing squad were almost immediate. On 20 May a large number of soldiers, many of them from the Monaghan Militia, attacked the offices of the *Northern Star* in Belfast. They assaulted the staff, destroyed the presses and threw the type into the street. The newspaper never appeared again. This was but the prelude to a concerted attempt to overawe the town. According to Samuel McSkimin, 'for weeks afterwards Belfast seemed as given up to licentious soldiery, whose destruction of private property appeared rather the acts of a savage mob, than those of an army levied for the support of good government, and the protection of the inhabitants.[49]

In the face of this repression, voices were raised demanding that the rebellion take place before the movement was completely destroyed.

There was a sharp difference of opinion over this issue within the United Irish leadership. A moderate faction favoured waiting until a successful landing by the French. This would have the advantage not only of ensuring a military victory, but also of containing the social radicalism that they feared a rising would inevitably unleash. This was the particular concern of Thomas Addis Emmet and William James MacNevin; indeed, it has been convincingly argued that they feared social revolution more than they feared defeat.[50] The moderates were opposed by more militant elements within the leadership: Arthur O'Connor, Edward Fitzgerald and Samuel Neilson. As far as they were concerned there was a real danger that the government's repressive measures would have destroyed the movement before the French arrived. There was considerable support for this view among the rank and file who were becoming increasingly impatient, waiting for the French while their backs were flogged and their homes burned. Hope gave voice to these sentiments, complaining of the 'foreign-aid men' who were always opposed to action. 'The people', he later recalled, 'wished to rise at various times, trusting solely to their own resources; but were always withheld by their committees, who were for the most part, aristocrats and foreign-aid men'. It was these elements in the leadership who were to provide the government with its spies and informers. He put his own success at avoiding arrest down to his refusal to have anything to do with them.[51]

Would a rising in June 1797, as was proposed, have had a serious chance of success? Certainly the United Irish movement was at its strongest at this point, although it had still made limited headway outside Ulster. Nevertheless, it was better armed and better organized than it was to be a year later, and still had its leadership intact. Moreover, 1797 was the year of the great Naval mutinies that, for a while at least, paralysed the British war effort. Irish seaman, many of them pressed into the Navy because of their rebel sympathies, played an important part in this episode. Indeed, Wolfe Tone was confident that sections of the British Fleet would have defected to the United Irish cause had the banner of revolt been raised. He was in no doubt that a great opportunity had been missed:

Five weeks, I believe six weeks, the English fleet was paralysed by mutinies in Portsmouth, Plymouth, and the Nore. The sea was open, and nothing to prevent both the Dutch and French fleets to put to sea. Well, nothing was ready, that precious opportunity, which we can never expect to return was lost ... Had we been in Ireland at the moment of the insurrection at the Nore, we should beyond a doubt, have had at least that fleet, and God only knows the influence which such an event might have had on the whole British navy. The destiny of Europe might have been changed forever.[52]

Later, he wrote in his *Journal* criticizing the United Irish leadership and its failure to stage a rising: 'there seems to me to have been a great want of spirit in the leaders in Dublin ... unpardonable weakness, if not downright cowardice to let such an occasion slip'.[53]

Repression and Rebellion

The methods that the British and Irish governments used in their efforts to destroy the United Irish movement were extremely brutal, amounting to a declaration of war against a hostile population. A deliberate and calculated decision was taken to cowe the Irish people by means of terror. The Viceroy, Lord Camden, was quite open about this, writing in November 1797 'that government meant to strike terror'.[54] Torture, the destruction of property and large-scale arrests were all made use of on a routine basis. The Irish Lord Chancellor, the much-hated Lord Fitzgibbon, defended torture Pinochet-style as 'necessary acts of severity' in the face of 'the fury of a fierce and savage democracy'.[55] One commentator noted light-heartedly that if the men of a village fled at the approach of troops then 'they whip the children and the ladies'.[56] Inevitably, when such methods were being carried out by poorly-disciplined troops of an often-Orange disposition they were accompanied by all manner of unofficial excesses, including rape and murder. The authorities effectively condoned this behaviour.

Historians, in recent years at least, have not made enough of the ferocity of the repression unleashed by the British. Too often it is played down or else balanced against acts of resistance carried out by the United Irishmen. The fact is, however, that as C. L. R. James pointed out many years ago in his marvellous study of the Haitian Revolt of the 1790s, 'property and privilege are always more ferocious than the revenges of poverty and oppression'.[57] This was certainly the case in Ireland. Let us briefly consider one particular episode from among many. In March 1797 United Irish prisoners on board the *Britannia* attempted to seize the ship off the coast of South America. They failed and eleven of them were subsequently flogged to death.[58] This atrocity is virtually unknown and goes without comment. If their mutiny had been successful and they had captured the ship and then proceeded to flog to death the ship's officers (something that they would never have even contemplated doing incidentally), can anyone seriously doubt that the atrocity would figure in every general account of the 1798 Rebellion. There is a double-standard operating whereby the deaths of ordinary people count for less than the deaths of people in authority. The point was actually made at the time (5 April 1798), when the Dublin Whig Club petitioned George III, urging him to protect the people from his government: 'Let us suppose a Lord Lieutenant picketed, Lords of the Council put to the torture, members of the two Houses sent to the fleet, their children hung up to extort confessions, their daughters ravished, and a bill of indemnity passed for the perpetrators of all this. What would be his Majesty's feelings on such an occasion?'.[59]

What is particularly interesting with regard to the repression in Ireland is that the conduct of the army was roundly condemned by the Commander-in-Chief, General Sir Ralph Abercromby, himself. This was quite unprecedented, but far from focusing the spotlight on the conduct of the troops, it has rather had the effect of marginalizing Abercromby, one of the most notable soldiers of the day. On 26 February 1798 he issued his famous order which condemned the army in Ireland for being 'in a state of licentiousness which must render it formidable to everyone but the enemy'. This indiscretion was to result in his enforced resignation. He was, in fact, considerably less restrained in his private correspondence. Here, he complained that the army had been ruined by 'the violence and oppression' of the Irish government, 'who have for more than twelve months employed it in measures which they durst not avow or sanction ... Within these twelve months, every crime, every cruelty that could be committed by Cossacks or Calmucks has been transacted here. The words of the order of February 26 were strong; the circumstances required it. It has not abated the commission of enormities ... Houses have been burned, men murdered, others half hanged. A young lady has been carried off by a detachment of dragoons ...'.[60]

Elsewhere he wrote that 'The abuses of all kinds I found here can scarcely be believed or enumerated'.[61]

Abercromby had no doubt as to the causes of the unrest in Ireland. It derived 'from the illiberal, the unjust, and the unwise conduct of England'. He went on to acknowledge the impact of 'the French Revolution and Jacobin principles ... yet the remote and ultimate cause must be derived from its true origin, the oppression of centuries'. Elsewhere he observed that the Irish ruling class 'know that they have been oppressors of the poor, and that the moment of vengeance is at hand'. As for the lower orders, they 'rejoice that in their opinion the moment is at hand when they can glut their revenge, and hope for a more equal share of the good things in life'.[62] Abercromby's indictment of the Irish establishment and its methods gets short shrift in the most recent revisionist history of the

Irish Yeomanry where he is summarily dismissed as having 'a doctrinaire approach to military matters'![63] And that is it.

What of the views of another eminent British soldier, who served in Ireland, General Sir John Moore? He was to become one of the great hero-martyrs of British Imperial history. According to Moore the procedure being followed in Ireland was to proclaim disturbed districts 'and to let loose the military, who were encouraged in acts of great violence against all who were supposed to be disaffected'. This certainly produced 'an apparent calm ... but the disaffection has been undoubtedly increased ... and a complete line seems to be drawn between the upper and lower orders'. On another occasion he complained that the government 'seem to have no plan or system but that of terrifying the common people: they will give you every power to act against them, but the rest of the community are to be indulged in every abuse'.[64] He asked to be relieved of his command, but his request was denied. Moore was to retain a reputation as one of the most humane British commanders throughout the Rebellion.

The intensity of the repression in Ulster together with the introduction of the new underground United Irish system in the South led to a shift in the movement's centre of gravity. This had already been evident as early as June 1797 when the national committee had rejected Ulster demands for an immediate rising. It was further symbolized by the effective suppression of the *Northern Star* in May 1797 and its replacement by Arthur O'Connor's Dublin revolutionary newspaper, the *Press*, in September of that year. According to Kevin Whelan the popularity of the *Press* was such that 'a crowd assembled on the night of publication in Church Lane to read each issue, amidst "a revelry of sedition".' To even possess a copy of the *Press* was to become a crime.[65] The movement was growing in Leinster with the organization consolidating and membership increasing in 'existing strongholds such as Dublin, Meath and Kildare' as well as extending 'into Wicklow, Carlow and Wexford, and to a lesser extent into the midland counties of Westmeath, King's and Queens'.[66] Nevertheless, the leadership in the South suffered a serious blow on 12 March 1798 when the Leinster provincial committee was arrested while meeting at Oliver Bond's house in Dublin. That same day, in separate raids, two members of the national committee, Thomas Addis Emmet and William James MacNevin were also taken. This certainly brought home to the government the extent of the threat they faced in Leinster (although the absence of the Wexford delegate led to an underestimation of the danger of that county), but ironically it also removed from the national leadership those men committed to postponing the rising. With the government intensifying its repression in the South, replacing the reluctant Abercromby as Commander-in-Chief with the more congenial Lake at the end of April, the demand for an insurrectionary response grew. The new leadership (Edward Fitzgerald, Samuel Neilson and the Sheares brothers, John and Henry) decided to wait no longer and prepared for a rising in May. The plan was for the rising to be launched in Dublin with the failure of the mail coaches to arrive providing the signal for the rest of the country. There is no doubt that Dublin's 10,000 sworn United Irishmen posed a serious threat and that a successful attempt, even with only part of the city falling into rebel hands, would have set the country alight.[67]

The plan miscarried. On 19 May the movement's military leader, Edward Fitzgerald, was arrested. He offered the most determined resistance, killing one of his attackers, seriously wounding another and finally being overpowered only after he had been shot. He was to die from his wounds on 4 June. The following day the government introduced martial law in Dublin and began filling the city with troops. On the 21st the Sheares brothers were arrested (they were both subsequently hanged) and the leadership of the rising was left in the hands of Samuel Neilson. The final timing was fixed for 10 p.m. on Wednesday 23 May. The government was forewarned and when the United Irishmen attempted to assemble, they found that troops had already occupied their rendezvous points, barricaded the bridges over the Liffey and set up checkpoints cutting communications with the surrounding countryside. Moreover, Neilson himself was captured, reconnoitring Newgate prison, with a view to storming it and to releasing the United Irish prisoners held there.

Even so the plan came near to success. According to Sir Richard Musgrave:

> It has been since discovered and proved, that the rebel drums were to have beaten to arms an hour after ours; and it is well known, that if they had preceded us by ever so small a space of time, the fate of the city and its loyal inhabitants would have been decided; for the mass of the people, armed with pikes and other weapons, were lurking in lanes, alleys and bye-places, ready to start forth on

the first beat of their drums, and would have occupied all the streets, and assassinated the yeomen before they could have reached their respective stations ...

As it was, large numbers of pikemen assembled in Church Street, Mary's Lane and Eccles Street and rebels armed with muskets took up positions in New Street, ready to ambush expected cavalry. Some 3,000 rebels came into the city from the surrounding countryside. With their leaders taken and with the city securely in the hands of the troops, the rising failed to take place and the rebels had dispersed by daybreak. Dublin had, once again in Musgrave's words, been saved from 'the licentious and destructive rage of the popish multitude' who would have assassinated all loyalists, violated their wives and plundered their property, by 'the seasonable discovery of the intended insurrection'.[68] The following days saw a regime of torture and summary execution imposed throughout the city.

Outside Dublin, United Irish forces mobilized during the night of 23 May with a view to reinforcing the rebels who, it was believed, would be fighting to seize the capital. While large numbers assembled in arms, there was no effective leadership and the various contingents were to be defeated piecemeal. The rebels suffered a number of setbacks culminating in heavy defeats at Kilcullen on 23 May, at Carlow on the 25th and at Tara on the 26th. In these engagements poorly-armed and badly-led rebel forces suffered heavy losses with the victorious troops enthusiastically carrying out General Lake's 'no prisoners' order. At Gibbet Rath over 300 unarmed United Irishmen attempting to surrender were massacred by troops on 29 May. In a way, even more shocking, in the village of Dunlavin, thirty-six prisoners arrested before the outbreak of the Rebellion were taken out and shot. A similar massacre of prisoners was carried out at Carnew.[69]

What rescued the Rebellion from an ignominious collapse was the United Irish victory over the North Cork Militia at Oulart Hill in County Wexford on 27 May. In the words of one historian, this 'was a stunning achievement by non-professional fighting men' and it opened the way for their domination of the entire county.[70] While the revolt failed elsewhere, in Wexford the rebels were able to establish a United Irish government, a revolutionary Directory consisting of four Protestants and four Catholics that offered 'a tantalizing brief glimpse of the potential had there been a successful United Irish coup in Dublin'.[71]

One last point is worth considering here: the attitude of the

Catholic Church towards the United Irish movement and the 1798 Rebellion. At the time, the Irish government and its apologists (mostly notably Sir Richard Musgrave) portrayed the Rebellion as a Catholic conspiracy to exterminate Protestantism. While not endorsing this view too many historians have lent credence to it by the emphasis they have placed on the sectarian atrocities committed by the rebel forces. All this is seriously misleading. The Catholic bishops led by Archbishop Troy completely and unreservedly sided with the Irish and British governments. In the words of Daire Keogh, the hierarchy mounted 'a full scale counter-revolutionary onslaught' against the so-called 'French Disease', culminating in excommunication. At the same time, it 'remained silent and voiced no protest at the suffering of the Catholic community'.[72] There can be little doubt that in such circumstances a United Irish victory would not have resulted in a Catholic Ascendancy, but rather in a revolution overwhelming the Church and sweeping away the loyalist bishops and clergy. While this might not have fulfilled the anti-clerical ambitions of the likes of Wolfe Tone,[73] it would certainly have ensured that a very different Catholic Church would have survived into the nineteenth century. As for the sectarian excesses carried out by the rebel forces, first, they were not always sectarian in motivation or character; second, they were condemned by the United Irish leadership; and third, they only occurred when discipline was beginning to break down and in response to the far worse excesses committed by government forces. Moreover, the sectarian behaviour and murderous conduct of the Crown forces, regular troops, yeomanry and militia, was deliberately condoned and encouraged by the Irish government as the surest way to defend itself against revolution. What is surprising given the nature of the Protestant Ascendancy is that there were not more episodes of Catholic sectarianism.

What of the handful of priests who threw in their lot with the United Irish cause? What is the significance of men such as James Coigley, a United Irish emissary, hanged on 7 June 1798 near Maidstone in Kent, and John Murphy, one of the leaders of Wexford Rising, flogged and hanged, his body burned and his head displayed on a pike on 2 July 1798 at Tullow.[74] According to Keogh some seventy priests took an active part in the Rising, about 4 per cent of the total, with the overwhelming majority either declaring for the government or remaining neutral.[75] While the many loyalists (including all the bishops) would undoubtedly have fled the country in the event of a United Irish victory, it is quite likely that many of those who remained neutral would have had no difficulty coming to terms with a revolutionary government made up of both Protestant and Catholic United Irishmen. Evidence to support this contention is provided by the large proportion of Irish priests ministering in France who were prepared to subscribe to the revolutionary Civil Constitution of the Clergy.[76] Even loyalism was not enough to save priests from Orange reprisals once the Rebellion had been crushed. John Redmond, a Wexford priest known as an 'orange priest' to his parishioners, went into hiding to escape the rebels. He emerged once they were beaten, only to be arrested by the yeomanry, flogged and publicly hanged with Lord Mountnorris firing his pistols into the suspended body.[77] Elsewhere, priests such as James Conry and Manus Sweeney were hanged not for any rebel sympathies but merely 'to strike terror into the hearts of the people by executing those who were most revered in their community'.[78] The temper of the Irish establishment and of their army is perhaps best captured by the appalled observations of Lord Cornwallis, an experienced soldier, who replaced Camden as Viceroy at the end of June 1798. 'The conversation even at my table', he wrote, 'where you will suppose I do all I can to prevent it, always turns on hanging, shooting, burning, etc., and if a priest has been put to death, the greatest joy is expressed by the whole company'. Our friends, he complained, have been 'endeavouring to make it a religions war', which, when added 'to the ferocity of our troops, who delight in murder', inevitably undermined any attempt at conciliation.[79]

The North Rises

The Belfast mail coach was successfully stopped at Santry, but the United Irish leaders in the North made no attempt at mobilization. They had been successfully intimidated by Lake's 'dragooning' and would not move without the French. Only pressure from below, from the rank and file, forced the County Antrim commander, Robert Simms to call a council to consider what action to take. The key figure here was James Hope, who convinced Simms that a revolt would take place anyway, with or without him. According to A. T. Q. Stewart, Hope was articulating the 'frustration, the impatience of the younger members of the organization with middle-aged leaders, and of working-class men with middle-class decisions'.[80] The provincial leadership was overthrown at a meeting on 29 May, provoking Simms and others into resignation. In effect, the United Irish leadership in Ulster abandoned the cause at the very moment they were called on to strike a blow. At a meeting of Antrim delegates on 3 June it was reported that the senior officers charged with leading the rising had all refused to turn out and after a heated debate the meeting voted to wait for the French. This decision produced uproar and the meeting broke up.

On their way home a number of the delegates stopped at the village of Ballyeaston to discuss the situation with the rank and file United Irishmen assembled there. They were—

... all anxious to learn of the decision of the day. On this being known, the crowd burst forth into an open uproar, and shouts of 'aristocrats', 'despots', 'cowards', 'villains' and even 'traitors' were heard from the multitude ... Amidst horrid threats and confusion, a meeting was convened anew, at which the Belfast gentleman presided, the decision at Sheepree was reversed, and the sovereign people declared they were appeased ... the day of insurrection was fixed upon ... the 7th June.[81]

The Belfast gentleman was Henry Joy McCracken.

According to Hope, the defection of the leaders left the United Irish movement in the North 'completely disorganized'. In the circumstances, their rebellion was more 'a forlorn hope, than a force having any well-founded expectation of a successful issue'.[82] Nevertheless, what is remarkable is the strength of the turn out. Nancy Curtin has estimated that despite 'such adverse circumstances, at least 27,000 men in Antrim, Down and east Derry actually took part in one or more engagement with government forces'.[83] The great majority of these men were Protestants. With more determined leadership and better organization, this force could have caused the British serious difficulties, and, of course, success would have rallied more men to the cause.

McCracken's intention was to seize Antrim town, where the county's magistrates were meeting, confident that their capture would cripple the loyalist cause. From here they could descend on Belfast and then, joining up with the rest of the Ulster United Irishmen, march on Dublin and link up with the Leinster rebels. He had no idea how badly the Rebellion had miscarried in the rest of the country with the exception of Wexford.

Rebel forces began to assemble in Antrim on the morning of 7 June with the first engagement taking place at Larne at 2 a.m. The garrison was driven from the town by a surprise attack whereupon the rebel force marched off to join up with McCracken. Other rebel contingents overwhelmed the garrisons at Randalstown and Ballymena, before converging on Donegore Hill overlooking Antrim town. By mid-afternoon, McCracken had over 4,000 men under his command with more still en route. According to one account this was the most substantial rebel army to take the field so far.[84] The town was held by some 300 troops who were reinforced by a party of dragoons. Although the United Irishmen had an overwhelming numerical superiority, McCracken faced the same problem that confronted the rebel forces everywhere: how to dislodge well-armed opponents from fortified positions with few firearms and no artillery. Even so they were nearly successful. At a crucial point, the dragoons were roughly handled and began to retreat, a retreat that would in all probability have turned into a rout, providing the Antrim rebels with their Oulart Hill. United Irish reinforcements approaching the town mistook the dragoons' retreat as an attack on themselves, broke and fled. With victory within their grasp, McCracken's men took the flight of their reinforcements as an indication that the battle was lost and began to withdraw themselves. The arrival of British reinforcements completed the defeat. All McCracken's efforts to rally his men and continue the attack failed and it was left to Hope and his pikemen to cover the retreat. Casualties in the fighting in the town had been light, with the rebels losing some twenty men killed, but in the pursuit that followed hundreds were killed, many of them unarmed and trying to surrender.[85] Hope quite correctly put the defeat down to McCracken's inability to control the battle, not that this was a personal failing, but rather that the wholesale defection of the leadership left him without any staff organization through which to exercise command. The various United Irish contingents were operating independently. McCracken did not have the means to co-ordinate his attack or to rally his men at the moment of crisis. A heavy price was to be paid.

While McCracken went on the run with a diminishing band of followers, the British proceeded with mopping up operations. Troops looted and pillaged friend and foe alike, burning houses, torturing suspects and summarily executing prisoners. The pacification climaxed with the burning of Randalstown. The British officer charged with this deed wrote: 'It fell to my lot to set fire to it ... The houses, being mostly thatch, were soon ablaze. Only those who witness such distressing scenes can form any idea of them'.[86]

Elsewhere in Ulster, large United Irish forces had assembled in County Derry and made an unsuccessful attack on Maghera. More substantial was the effort in County Down which got under way on 9 June with an attack on Saintfield. Led by Henry Munro, the rebels were eventually defeated at Ballynahinch on 12 June with some 500 men killed in the fighting and the pursuit. There followed what A. T. Q. Stewart describes as 'a brief reign of terror' and Charles Dickson as 'the period of uncontrolled savagery'.[87] House burnings, torture, shootings and hangings. On 11 August 1798 the Dublin newspaper, the *Freeman's Journal,* observed: 'the magnitude of the punishment of many districts in County Down may be conceived from this single fact: that of the inhabitants of the little village of Ballywalter in the Ardes, nine men were actually killed and thirteen returned wounded, victims of their folly. If a trifling village suffered so much what must have been the aggregate loss ...'.[88] The Northern Rising was over

Henry Munro was hanged on 16 June, but the authorities had considerable difficulty obtaining witnesses to convict McCracken. One of his English workmen, William Thompson, was almost flogged to death in an attempt to get him to implicate McCracken. In the event, he had to be convicted on the perjured evidence of two paid informers whom he had never seen before. He was hanged on 17 July. Hope provides a testimonial for his executed comrade:

> when all our leaders deserted us, Henry Joy McCracken stood alone, faithful to the last ... He died rather than prove a traitor to his cause of which fact I am still a living witness, who shared in all his exertions while he lived, and defy any authentic contradiction of that assertion now or at any future date.[89]

Aftermath

The United Irish revolt in Wexford was inevitably crushed once the British were able to concentrate their forces against it. The most ferocious repression followed with rape, pillage and murder the order of the day. Many rebels escaped into the Wicklow mountains and, led by men such as Joseph Holt and Michael Dwyer, continued a guerrilla war that lasted into the early years of the next century.

Only after the defeat of the Wexford rebels did the French

finally arrive in the shape of a small expedition of some 1,000 men under General Humbert. They landed in north Mayo on 22 August and were joined by thousands of United Irish rebels who had so far played no part in events. Once again, the British were able to concentrate overwhelming forces against them. Humbert finally surrendered on 8 September. His French troops were treated as prisoners-of-war, but his Irish allies were massacred. Hundreds were killed on the spot and many more were hunted down in the days that followed. Those who were, in the end, made prisoners were forced to draw lots to see who should be executed.[90] Among the French officers captured were two United Irish exiles, Mathew Tone and Bartholomew Teeling, who were both hanged.

The last act occurred in October when another French naval expedition attempted to land 3,000 troops under General Hardy. They were intercepted at sea. Among those captured was Wolfe Tone. He was sentenced to hang on 11 November 1798 but cut his own throat in prison, dying on the 19th. Lord Chancellor Fitzgibbon could not understand why he was not hanged regardless, 'severed throat and all'.[91]

What of James Hope? He escaped arrest in the aftermath of the June defeats. Partly this was due to his ability to disappear into the working class and partly it was due to the fact that he always went armed and was determined not to be taken alive. His own account provides dramatic testimony to the dangerous nature of the times. Nevertheless, he remained wholeheartedly committed to the United Irish cause, and when the movement was reorganized under the leadership of Robert Emmet and Thomas Russell once again became a key emissary. It was Hope who established contact with Dwyer's guerrillas in the Wicklow mountains, supplying them with weapons and who, together with Russell, revived the movement in the North.[92] Recent research has clearly established that the 1803 conspiracy was a far more substantial affair than was traditionally believed. Hope himself was involved in preparations for a rebel attack on Ballymena, but a general Rising never took place. Instead, Emmet staged his futile demonstration on 23 July.[93] Nancy Curtin has convincingly argued that even at this late stage, if Emmet had been able to seize Dublin, 'the North might well have risen formidably again'.[94] It was not to be. Emmet was hanged on 20 September 1803 and Russell a month later on 20 October. The United Irish movement never recovered.

Once again, Hope went on the run and successfully avoided arrest. In his own words, 'nothing remained for me but to baffle the designs of the enemy against myself. I went about armed for three years, determined never to be taken alive'.[95] He lived out the rest of his life as a working man, remaining both a Protestant and a Republican, committed to social equality and social justice, and to the interests of working people, both Catholic and Protestant. His autobiography is a tremendous account of his life and times and a vital contribution to our understanding of the United Irish movement, the most important revolutionary movement in modern British and Irish history.

A Note on R. R. Madden

Richard Madden was born in Dublin on 20 August 1798, according to his own account, while the house was actually being searched for arms. He trained as a doctor and travelled extensively in the Middle East, publishing a two-volume work, *Travels in Turkey, Egypt, Nubia and Palestine* in 1829. Subsequently, he settled in London and became active in the Anti-Slavery movement. In 1833 he was sent to Jamaica as a special magistrate to help superintend the abolition. He was appointed to an Anglo-Spanish Commission investigating the slave trade and this led to his giving evidence at the celebrated *Amistad* trial in the United States.[96] While in the United States, he met United Irish exiles and began to collect the material that eventually made up his seven volume *United Irishmen: Their Lives and Times* and a number of other volumes, *Literary Remains of the United Irishmen* and *Antrim and Down in '98* from which Hope's autobiography is taken. It was Madden who 'discovered' Wolfe Tone's neglected grave at Bodenstown in 1842. He was sympathetic to the Young Ireland movement in the 1840s and was apparently himself under police surveillance for a while.[97] Through Henry Joy McCracken's sister, Mary Ann, he met James Hope and they became close friends.[98] Hope, by now, in his eighties, was living in poverty, but with his spirit unbroken. When he died in 1847, Madden together with Israel Milkeen and Mary Ann McCracken had a memorial erected on his grave:

erected
to the memory of
JAMES HOPE
who was born in 1764 and died in 1847
one of nature's noblest works
AN HONEST MAN
steadfast in faith and always hopeful
of divine protection
in the best era of his country's history
a soldier in her cause
and at the worst times still faithful to it
ever true to himself and to those
who trusted in him, he remained to the last
unchanged and unchangeable
in his fidelity.[99]

Notes

[1] Kevin Whelan, *The Tree of Liberty: Radicalism, Catholicism and the Construction of Irish Identity 1760–1830*, Cork, Cork University, 1996, p. ix.
[2] Nancy J. Curtin, *The United Irishmen: Popular Politics in Ulster and Dublin 1791–1798*, Oxford, Oxford University Press, 1994, p. 259.
[3] A. T. Q. Stewart, *The Summer Soldiers: The 1798 Rebellion in Antrim and Down*, Belfast, the Blackstaff Press, 1995, p. 61.
[4] Charles Hamilton Teeling, *History of the Irish Rebellion of 1798*, Shannon, Irish University Press, 1972, p. 126.
[5] For the foundation of the United Irish Society in Belfast see Marianne Elliott, *Partners in Revolution: the United Irishmen and France*, New Haven, Yale University Press, 1982, pp. 22–23. For Wolfe Tone see her *Wolfe Tone: Prophet of Irish Independence*, New Haven, Yale University Press, 1989.
[6] R. B. McDowell, *Ireland in the Age of Imperialism and Revolution 1760–1801*, Oxford, Oxford University Press, 1979, p. 387.
[7] See Maureen Wall, 'The rise of a Catholic middle class in eighteenth-century Ireland', *Irish Historical Studies*, 11, 42 September 1958.
[8] For an excellent account of this first Catholic Emancipation campaign see Jim Smyth, *The Men of No Property: Irish Radicals and Popular Politics in the Late Eighteenth Century*, Basingstoke, Macmillan 1994, pp. 52–78.
[9] Gillian O'Brien, 'Spirit, Impartiality and Independence: *The Northern Star* 1792–1797', *Eighteenth Century Ireland*, 13, 1998.
[10] Simon Davies, 'The Northern Star and the propagation of enlightened ideas' *Eighteenth Century Ireland*, 5, 1990, p. 150.
[11] Whelan, op. cit., p. 69.
[12] Curtin, op. cit., p. 60.
[13] See the discussion in Smyth, op. cit., p. 98.
[14] Elliott, *Partners in Revolution*, op. cit., p. 67–68.
[15] For the reorganization of the United Irishmen see Curtin, op. cit., pp. 90–116.
[16] For the Defenders see Smyth, op. cit., pp. 1000–120. See also Thomas Bartlett, 'Select documents: Defenders and Defenderism in 1795', *Irish Historical Studies* 24, 96 1985.

[17] James Hope, *Autobiography*, p. 50. All future references are to the text in this volume.

[18] Jim Smyth, 'Dublin's Political Underground in the 1790s' from Gerard O'Brien, *Parliament, Politics and People*, Dublin, Irish Academic Press 1989, p. 135. See also David A. Wilson, *United Irishmen, United States: Immigrant Radicals in the early Republic*, Dublin, Four Courts Press, 1998, p. 23.

[19] Hope, p. 56.

[20] Smyth, *The Men of No Property*, op. cit., p. 142.

[21] For the Bantry Bay expedition and its significance see J. A. Murphy ed., *The French Are In the Bay: The Expedition to Bantry Bay 1796*, Dublin, Mercier Press, 1997.

[22] Thomas Bartlett, ed., *Life of Theobald Wolfe Tone: Memoirs, journals and political writings, compiled and arranged by William T. W. Tone, 1826* Dublin, the Lilliput Press, 1998, p. 669.

[23] W. E. H. Lecky, *A History of Ireland in the Eighteenth Century* IV, London, Longmans, Green and Co, 1913, p. 3.

[24] Sir Richard Musgrave, *Memoirs of the Different Rebellions in Ireland*, Fort Wayne, Indiana, Round Tower Books, 1995, p. 134–135. For a recent discussion of Musgrave see Jim Smyth, 'Anti-Catholicism, Conservatism and Conspiracy: Sir Richard Musgrave's *Memoirs of the Different Rebellions in Ireland*', *Eighteenth Century Life*, 22, 3 November 1998.

[25] Nancy J. Curtin, 'Ideology and Materialism: Politicization and Ulster Weavers in the 1790s' from Marilyn Cohen, *The Warp of Ulster's Past*, Basingstoke, Macmillan, 1997, p. 119.

[26] Arthur O'Connor (James Livesey ed.) *The State of Ireland*, Dublin, the Lilliput Press, 1998, pp. 9, 34, 37, 66–67, 122. See also Frank Macdermott, 'Arthur O'Connor', *Irish Historical Studies*, 15, 57, 1966.

[27] See discussion in Smyth, *Men of No Property*, op. cit., pp. 164–165.

[28] Ibid., pp. 145–146.

[29] James Quinn, 'The United Irishmen and social reform', *Irish Historical Studies*, 31, 122 November 1998, pp. 192, 193.

[30] C. J. Woods, ed., *Journals and Memoirs of Thomas Russell*, Dublin, Irish Academic Press, 1991, pp. 82, 88, 139. See also Denis Carroll, *The Man from God Knows Where: Thomas Russell 1767–1803*, Blackrock, Gartan 1995, and Brendan Clifford, *Thomas Russell and Belfast*, Belfast, Athol Books, 1997.

[31] Hope, pp. 47, 53, 55, 59. It has been suggested by Ian McBride that Hope's opinions might owe more to the British Chartism of the 1840s than to the Irish Jacobinism of the 1790s. Some sort of continuity seems more likely. Certainly his own account provides ample testimony to the social radicalism of elements within the United Irish movement:

'As the new popular societies emerged, however, grievances were focussed much more sharply on the inequalities of the social order. One oath found in Newry early in 1797 declared that the United Irishmen would "join the French on landing and pull down all Gentleman and Magistrates, Tithes, Taxes and Rents, etc." ...'

From I. R. McBride, *Scripture Politics* Oxford, Oxford University Press, 1998, pp. 901, 181–182.

[32] Elliott, *Partners in Revolution*, op. cit., p. XVIII.

[33] See, in particular, Roger Wells, *Insurrection: The British Experience 1795–1803* Gloucester, Alan Sutton 1983; E. W. McFarland, *Ireland and Scotland in the Age of Revolution*, Edinburgh, Edinburgh University Press, 1994; and Martin J. Mitchell, *The Irish in the West of Scotland 1797–1848: Trade Unions, Strikes and Political Movements*, Edinburgh, John Donald, 1998.

[34] Elliott, *Partners in Revolution*, op. cit., 149–150.

[35]   Curtin, *The United Irishmen*, op. cit., p. 125.

[36]   Brendon McEvoy, 'The United Irishmen in County Tyrone', *Seanchas Ardmhacha* 3 1957, 4 1960–61, 6 1969. See also Bréandon Mac Suibhne, 'Up Not Out: Why did North-West Ulster Not Rise in 1798' from Cathal Póirtéir, *The Great Irish Rebellion of 1798*, Cork, Mercier Press 1998.

[37]   Whelan, op. cit., 75, 85, 86–88.

[38]   Lecky, op. cit., p. 29.

[39]   Ibid., pp. 40–41.

[40]   Ibid., pp. 39–40, 50.

[41]   For the Orange Order see Hereward Senior, *Orangeism in Ireland and Britain 1795–1836*, London, Routledge, Kegan Paul, 1966.

[42]   Lecky, op. cit., 52, 53, 55.

[43]   Thomas Bartlett, 'Defence, counter-insurgency and rebellion: Ireland 1793–1803' in Thomas Bartlett and Keith Jeffery, eds., *A Military History of Ireland*, Cambridge, Cambridge University Press, 1996, p. 262.

[44]   Even Smyth, *Men of No Property*, op. cit., p. 172 accepts this argument.

[45]   McDowell, op. cit., p. 470.

[46]   Whelan, op. cit., p. 119.

[47]   Stewart, op. cit., p. 39.

[48]   See Thomas Bartlett, 'Indiscipline and disaffection in the armed forces in Ireland in the 1790s' in Patrick J. Corish, *Radicals, Rebels and Establishments*, Belfast, Appletree Press 1985.

[49]   Samuel McSkimin, *Annals of Ulster*, Belfast, James Cleeland, 1906, p. 52.

[50]   Curtin, *The United Irishmen*, op. cit., pp. 87–88.

[51]   Hope, p. 66.

[52]   Bartlett, *Life of Theobald Wolfe Tone*, op. cit., p. 796.

[53]   Ibid., pp. 797–798.

[54]   Bartlett, 'Defence, counter-insurgency and rebellion', op. cit., p. 270.

[55]   Ann C. Kavanaugh, *John Fitzgibbon, Earl of Clare*, Dublin, Irish Academic Press, 1997, p. 334.

[56]   Thomas Bartlett, *The Rise and Fall of the Irish Nation*, Dublin, Gill and Macmillan, 1992, p. 231.

[57]   C. L. R. James, *The Black Jacobins: Toussaint Louverture and the San Domingo Revolution*, London, Allison and Busby 1980 pp. 88–89.

[58]   Ruan O'Donnell, *1798 Diary*, Dublin, Irish Times Books, 1998, p. 18.

[59]   Charles Dickson, *Revolt in the North: Antrim and Down in 1798*, London, Constable, 1997, p. 120.

[60]   James, Lord Dunfermiline, *Lieutenant-General Sir Ralph Abercromby: A Memoir*, Edinburgh, Edmonstone and Douglas, 1861 pp. 93–94, 108.

[61]   Lecky, op. cit., p. 210.

[62]   Dunfermline, op. cit., pp. 127, 129.

[63]   Allan Blackstock, *An Ascendancy Army: The Irish Yeomanry 1796–1834*, Dublin, Four Courts Press, 1998, pp. 143–144.

[64]   J. F. Maurice, ed., *The Diary of Sir John Moore* I, London, Edward Arnold, 1904, pp. 271, 288.

[65]   Whelan, op. cit., pp. 70–71.

[66]   Thomas Graham, ' "An Union of Power"? The United Irish Organization 1795–1798' in David Dickson, Daire Keogh and Kevin Whelan, eds., *The United Irishmen: Republicanism, Radicalism and Rebellion*, Dublin, the Lilliput Press, 1993, p. 248.

[67]   See in particular Thomas Graham, 'Dublin's Role in the 1798 Rebellion' in Póirtéir, op. cit.

[68]   Musgrave, op. cit., pp. 192, 197.

JAMES HOPE, THE UNITED IRISHMEN AND 1798

[69] See Chris Lawlor, *The Massacre on Dunlavin Green: A Story of the 1798 Rebellion*, Naas, C. Lawlor, 1998.

[70] Kevin Whelan, 'Reinterpreting the 1798 Rebellion in County Wexford' in Daire Keogh and Nicholas Furlong, *The Mighty Wave: The 1798 Rebellion in Wexford*, Blackrock, Four Courts Press, 1996, p. 24. On the Wexford Rebellion see also Daniel Gahan, *The People's Rising: Wexford 1798*, Dublin, Gill and Macmillan, 1995. For a stimulating dissident view see Tom Dunne, 'Rebel Motives and Mentalities: The Battle for New Ross, 5 June 1798', *Eire–Ireland*, 34, 2 Summer 1999.

[71] Whelan, ibid., p. 25.

[72] Daire Keogh, *The French Disease: the Catholic Church and Radicalism in Ireland 1790–1800*, Dublin, Four Courts Press, 1993, pp. 101–102, 136. See also Vincent J. McNally, *Reform, Revolution and Reaction: Archbishop John Thomas Troy and the Catholic Church in Ireland 1787–1817*, New York, University Press of America, 1995.

[73] Wolfe Tone, of course, on 1 March 1798 enthusiastically welcomed the downfall of the Pope:
'An event has taken place of a magnitude scarce, if at all, inferior in importance to that of the French Revolution. The Pope is dethroned and in exile. The circumstances relating to this great event are such as to satisfy my mind that there is a special Providence guiding the affairs of Europe at this moment, and turning every thing to the great end of the emancipation of mankind from the yoke of religious and political superstition under which they have so long groaned'.— *Life of Theobald Wolfe Tone*, op. cit., p. 825.

[74] See Daire Keogh, ed., *A Patriot Priest: the Life of Father James Coigley*, Cork, Cork University Press, 1998, and Nicholas Furlong, *Fr. John Murphy of Boolavogue 1753–1798*, Dublin, Geography Publications, 1991.

[75] Keogh, *The French Disease*, op. cit., pp. 159–160. At least some of the seventy were the victims of Protestant reprisals rather than actual participants in the Rebellion.

[76] Philippe Loupès, 'The Irish Clergy of the Diocese of Bordeaux during the Revolution', from Hugh Gough and David Dickson, *Ireland and the French Revolution*, Dublin, The Four Courts Press, 1990.

[77] Kevin Whelan, 'The Role of the Catholic Priest in the 1798 Rebellion is County Wexford' in Kevin Whelan, ed., *Wexford: History and Society*, Dublin, Geography Publications, 1987, p. 31.

[78] Sheila Mulloy, 'The Clergy and the Connacht Rebellion' in Liam Swords, ed., *Protestant, Catholic and Dissenter: The Clergy and 1798*, Blackrock, the Columbia Press, 1997, p. 267.

[79] W. E. H. Lecky, *A History of Ireland in the Eighteenth Century*, 5, London, Longmans, Green and Co., 1913, pp. 14–5.

[80] Stewart, op. cit., p. 62.

[81] McSkibin, op. cit., p.70.

[82] Hope, pp. 99, 104.

[83] Curtin, *The United Irishmen*, op. cit., p. 277.

[84] Daniel Gahan, *Rebellion! Ireland in 1798*, Dublin, the O'Brien Press, 1998, p. 69.

[85] For the best account of the battle see Stewart, op. cit., pp. 102–121.

[86] Ibid., p. 155.

[87] Ibid., p. 232; Dickson, *Revolt in the North*, op. cit., p. 157.

[88] Dickson, ibid., p. 157.

[89] Hope, p. 76.

[90] Liam Kelly, *A flame Now Quenched: Rebels and Frenchmen in Leitrim 1793–1798*, Dublin, the Lilliput Press, 1998, p. 129.

41

[91] Kavanaugh, op. cit., p. 350.

[92] Ruan O'Donnell, *Aftermath: Post-Rebellion Insurgency in Wicklow 1799–1803*, Dublin, Irish Academic Press, 2000, pp. 120–123; Carroll, op. cit., pp. 167–174.

[93] For the best account of Emmet and the 1803 attempt at Rebellion see Elliott, *Partners in Revolution*, op. cit., pp. 282–322.

[94] Nancy J. Curtin, 'Rebels and Radicals: the United Irishmen in County Down' in Lindsay Proudfoot, *Down: History and Society*, Dublin, Geography Publications, 1997, p. 290. See also James G. Patterson, 'Continued Presbyterian Resistance in the Aftermath of the Rebellion of 1798 in Antrim and Down', *Eighteenth Century Life* 22, 3 November 1998.

[95] Hope, p. 92.

[96] For the *Amistad* affair see Howard Jones, *Mutiny on the Amistad*, Oxford, Oxford University Press, 1987.

[97] For Madden see Leon Ó Broin, 'R. R. Madden, Historian of the United Irishmen' *Irish University Review*, 2, 1972.

[98] For a recent discussion of Mary Ann McCracken see John Gray, 'Mary Ann McCracken: Belfast revolutionary and pioneer of feminism' in Nicholas Furlong and Daire Keogh, *The Women of 1798*, Dublin, Four Courts Press, 1998, pp. 47–63.

[99] Michael O'Flanagan, *When they Followed Henry Joy*, Dublin, Riposte Books, 1997, p. 18.

Introduction

'Master, go on, and I will follow thee
To the last gasp, with truth and loyalty.'
As you like it—Act II. Sc. 3.

In the following narrative, James Hope, a native of Temple-patrick, in the North of Ireland—a poor mechanic, self-taught and self-ennobled, now verging on his eighty-first year, has told his own story, recorded his own acts and opinions; and the duty which devolved on me was, to reduce to order a mass of unconnected materials, piled on one another in reference to events, not in the order of their succession, but as passing circumstances or topics of conversation chanced to recall them. The labour which this duty imposed, was sufficiently arduous. With the arrangement of those materials, their orthography and grammar, I have taken the liberty of dealing, as it seemed to me the disinternment of the sense required. It only remains for me to add a few words, as to my own opinions of the character and mental qualities of the writer of the narrative, calculated, I think, to show that no ordinary powers of mind were bestowed on this illiterate man.

James Hope, one of nature's nobility, and one of the finest specimens of 'his order' whom I ever met with, is a poor weaver, living in Belfast, not in absolute poverty, but in very humble circumstances. My first interview with him was at the house of a man of his own class, and one of his own stamp— Israel Milliken, of Belfast. Nothing could be more unpromising than our first acquaintance. I have reason to feel proud, how-ever, of having appreciated the man's worth, under discouraging circumstances, of having obtained his confidence, and got the better of his reserve on the second occasion of our coming together. To that circumstance, is due the publication of the following narrative. He is now in his eighty-first year—hale, hearty, cheerful, and steadfast in his early principles and opinions. Though bent with age, and impaired in bodily vigour, his gait, his frame, his deportment, still give the idea of a man who had been fitted to endure fatigue and hardship, and moulded for emergencies in which great activity and energy of mind and body were requisite to his safety, or that of others.

His wife died in Belfast some fifteen or sixteen years ago. He seldom speaks of her; but when he does, it seems as if he felt her spirit was hovering over him, and that it was not permitted to him to give expression to the praise which rises to his lips when her name is mentioned. There is something of refinement—rare as it is pleasing to contemplate, in the nature of his attachment—in the ties which bound him to that amiable, exemplary, and enthusiastic creature; for such she is represented to have been by those who knew her, amongst whom, was Miss M'Cracken, of Belfast.

Hope is a modest, observant, though retiring man, discreet and thoughtful. His height is about five feet seven inches, his frame slight but compact, his features remarkable for the tranquility and simplicity of their expression. His spirits seem to undergo no change: he is always in good humour, gay without levity, and yet laughter appears seldom to go beyond his eyes. His private character is most excellent: he is strictly moral, utterly fearless, inflexible, and incorruptible. The most eminent leaders, both of 1798 and 1803, had a thorough confidence in him. He was always temperate, moderate in his desires, and industrious in his habits. I have had personal experience of the independence of his principles; to no man would he be indebted for his opinions or his comforts. He is a self-taught man, of the most clear and vigorous intellect; fond of reading history, of the lives and maxims especially of ancient philosophers, and of the application of the latter to modern times. For a term of upwards of sixty years he has earned his bread by his own industry; strictly honourable in his dealings and in his connections; he is unalterable in his attachments, faithful to his promises, fearless of every consequence in the performance of his duty to his friends and to his country. He is a man of very profound reflection. His courage has been tried on numerous occasions: his fidelity to his associates no less often—to Neilson, M'Cracken, Emmet, Russell, and Hamilton. He was at all times adverse to bloodshed. His mind seems so constructed as to make it impossible for him to feel or manifest any respect for men, whatever may be their station, except on account of their good or noble qualities. He treats of events in which he was an actor, as if his only anxiety was for the fame of his associates, and his only object had been to promote their common cause. He is perfectly conscious, however, of his intellectual powers.

R. R. Madden

CHAPTER I

I WAS BORN in the Parish of Templepatrick, in the County Antrim, the 25th August, 1764. My father was a native of the Parish of Templepatrick, he was a Highlander, a refugee, one of the Covenanters. He followed the linen-weaving business, and brought me up to it. My parents died at Templepatrick, and were buried at Molusk. They were simple honest people, Presbyterians, and their children were brought up in that religion, chiefly under the ministry of the Rev. Isaac Patten, near Lisle Hill. I had two brothers who grew up to manhood, one of whom is still living. By the time I was ten years of age I had been fifteen weeks at school, and this was all the day school learning I ever received.

The first three years I earned my bread, was with William Bell, of Templepatrick, who took every opportunity, of improving my mind, that my years would admit. In winter he made me get forward my work, and sit with him while he read in the histories of Greece and Rome, and also Ireland, Scotland, and England; besides his reading and comments on the news of the day, turned my attention early to the nature of the relations between the different classes of society, and passing events rather left impressions on my mind for future examinations, than established any particular opinions.

After some time I was taken from Bell, and hired to a farmer named John Gibson, in the same parish. His father, a small farmer, was still alive, and from this venerable old man, I received a great deal of good instruction, which confirmed my first impressions of a religious nature. I had learned to spell, and he set me to read and write, but he died before I had made much progress. I served half a year with another farmer, named John Ritchy, who gave me a little more help in writing; and afterwards returning to my former master, he assisted me in reading, until I could read a little in the Bible, though very imperfectly.

At length I was apprenticed to a linen weaver, and I served my full time to him without reproof. On leaving my old master I entered into an engagement with a small farmer who had a loom in his house, at which I wrought, for eight years and a half, during which time I improved in reading and writing by attending a night school during the winter seasons. I subsequently worked as a journeyman weaver with a man of the name of Mullen, and married the daughter of my employer, Rose Mullen, a young woman gifted with noble qualities, with every advantage of mind and person, she was every thing in this world to me, and when I lost her, my happiness went to the grave with her. She died in 1831. I had four children who grew up, two of whom are now living.

From an early age my mind was directed to public affairs. I attended public worship with the members of a seceding congregation in the Parish of Templepatrick, in the County of Antrim, in which there were then two congregations, one in the village where the Rev. John Abernethy was minister, and the other near Lile Hill, taught by the Rev. Isaac Patten, where I was baptized. One day I heard Mr Patten explaining the 83rd Psalm, and praying for the down-fall of Turk and Anti-Christ, and for the purging of the blood that lay unpurged, on the throne of Britain, and also for the down-fall of Pope and Popery, which latter prayer composed part of his devotions every Sabbath. But when the Royal Bounty was extended to our ministers, then the destruction of Pope and Popery became the principal supplication of the poor northern sinners to the throne of divine grace; the throne of Britain, according to the fanatical notions of those times, was purged and purified in the smoke of the blood then beginning to be shed in the woods of America, and in fairs and markets in Ireland, particularly in the County Armagh; then Mr Patten began praying for the stoppage of the effusion of *Protestant blood*, but from the impression of his former instructions on my mind, I used to think of the stoppage of the effusion of *human blood* when attempting to join him in prayer.

These thoughts began to expand, when I saw the regiments of fine looking fellows, driving off to be slaughtered in America, and heard 'the break of day men' boasting of the indulgence they got from magistrates for wrecking and beating the papists, as they called their neighbours, and the snug bits of land that their friends got when the papists fled to Connaught, and the fun they had, when committing depredations, for which warrants lay out against them, of which they had, always notice, in time to escape. Our parish was inhabited by settlers from Scotland, some of whom had fled from persecution in their own country, of which my grandfather was one.

When King William landed, they joined his interest, and dreaded the natives, of course, who had all left our parish but two families of the names of Niell and Tolan, who were servants in Castle Upton during the siege of Derry, and respected by the Upton family for many years for their fidelity during that war.

The Parish of Templepatrick was thus cleared of all the natives who were Catholics, and was very thinly inhabited, even within my own memory, to what it is now. The republican spirit, inherent in the principles of the Presbyterian community, kept resistance to arbitrary power still alive, though selfishness prevented its proper direction, and induced men to do to 'others what they would resist if done to themselves.'

The American struggle taught people, that industry had its rights as well as aristocracy, that one required a guarantee, as well as the other; which gave extension to the forward view of the Irish leaders. The war commenced between the claims of the plough and the sword, fiction became arrayed against reality, the interests of capital against those of labour, and the rich lost sight of their dependence on the poor. Society was disjointed, and there was no guarantee for the preservation of the rights of industry. The claims founded on fiction, however, predominated, and ranks arose in such disproportion that mankind seemed divided into different species, each preying on the other; from necessity, with the exception of a few enlightened men, in every rank, who deprecated those evils, and looked forward to a better state of things.

Until the commencement of the contest with the United States, foreign war had encouraged industry at home, but the difficulty of recruiting for our armies in America, suggested an unnatural expedient. 'Discourage the linen trade,' said the then Lord Hillsborough, 'and you will have soldiers.' The plan succeeded and the linen weavers suffered. Every other branch in Ulster felt the depression, and until machinery was introduced, trade continued low. The cotton manufacture, however, succeeded the linen one, and many of the hands that it had employed joined the former.

The Volunteers of 1782 were the means of breaking the first link of the penal chain that bound Ireland. They were replaced by the Break-of-day robbers, the wreckers, and murderers, who were supported by an indemnified magistracy; and the system which grew out of these combinations, comprehends the political history of Ireland from 1782 down to a later period in the history of Orangeism.

The blood of Ireland has been abundantly shed during that period, at home and abroad. Those who profited by this system, and were privy to it, are not guiltless of murder—*and who were they*—every man of mature age during that period, who did not use all his rational powers to prevent that mischief, who connived at it, who encouraged, or permitted it to be encouraged, who shared in the temporary plunder or adopted the policy of sowing dissentions, with the view of reaping temporary or supposed advantages to the governing powers.

My connection with politics began in the ranks of the Volunteers; I was a member of the Roughford corps. Of the first founders of the United Societies only two were intimately known to me—Mr Samuel Neilson and Henry Joy M'Cracken. I lived in the country when I joined the society, and was delegated to a committee in Belfast, where I met them. Some time after I met Mr Thomas Russell. There was a rule, then in the societies, that required seven to constitute a society; and, when constituted, every additional member was proposed and ballotted for at one meeting, and admitted at the next. Mr Russell told me that he took the test from James Agnew O'Farrell, of Larne, when he was admitted to the society.

June 26th, 1795, I was met by a neighbour, who told me that a political society was being formed; that the members were chosen by ballot; that I had been approved of, if I was willing to join; that there was a declaration to be made, and a test or oath to be taken, of which, if I did not approve, I was told I might decline to take it, on condition that I would not divulge any thing concerning the society. We talked on the subject for some time, during which I lamented that we should shrink from an open declaration of our views into conspiracy; that oaths would never bind rogues, that I would rather act openly, in which way of proceeding, there was but one danger. I was told that my neighbours would not go with me in this view of matters, and it was necessary to know, would I go with them. 'I will not desert my neighbours,' said I, 'though I do not like the road; I'll travel it, however, as clean as I can.' By the direction of the man referred to, I attended the next meeting; the declaration I felt to be true; I voluntarily conformed to the rules of the society, and joined it with heart and hand. A deputation from Belfast formed the Molusk society, of which I became a member, the Hightown society having been that in which I was initiated, and composed of the men I had first joined in arms as a volunteer.

I was delegated to a committee in Belfast, and when the baronial committees were formed, I was appointed a delegate to the upper half barony of Belfast; there was a committee in every half barony.

I was not qualified for public speaking; my mind was like Swift's church, the more that was inside, the slower the mass came out; my comrades called me the Spartan. My motives for joining the United Irishmen were, to carry out the objects of the volunteers; my first views were not beyond theirs; they became more extensive. The person who induced me to join the society is still living. I was employed in 1796, 1797, and the spring of 1798, and again in 1803, as an emissary, going from place to place throughout the country, organizing the people. I received my orders generally from Russell, Wilson, and M'Cracken, and communicated with several persons, I was sworn never to name; also with John M'Cann, and Edward Dunn, foreman in Jackson's foundry, who had a very close acquaintance with the views of the Directory. In my own society, in the north, I held the office of delegate to the county committee. I was in the confidence of the Ulster Director, and of some of the principal members of the Leinster one. I took the oath of an United Irishman by being sworn on the Bible; the Covenanters were sworn by lifting up the right hand; the Catholics on their own prayer-book.

Manufacture and commerce sprung up rapidly, and corrupt and interested views increased in variety and complication. The manufacturer had two strings to his bow, while the mere cultivator of the soil had but one, and that one only during the landlord's pleasure. The younger branches of his family either learned some trade, or became day-labourers. Such as were prudent and industrious, rented cottages from the farmers, and were able to offer a higher rent to the landlord, at the end of the farmer's tenure, which completely destroyed good will between them. This was the real source of the persecution in the County Armagh, religious profession being only a pretext to banish a Roman Catholic from his snug little cottage, or spot of land, and get possessed of it. The sufferers were forced into associations, in defence of life and property, directed by a committee, which they agreed to obey. This association was for a time confined to those professing the Roman Catholic religion, but the members joined eventually the cause of their Protestant fellow-countrymen, and became sworn brothers. This plan of union was projected by Neilson, assisted by Luke Teeling of Lisburn, and his family and connection, being a linen merchant of the first rank, and a Roman Catholic, who never came under any oath or obligation to the society, but that of conscientious approval.

While Tone and Neilson were endeavouring to establish the United Irish societies in Belfast, young Charles Teeling was labouring in the meantime to unite the Defenders and Catholics of the smaller towns of Ulster; and even the Break-of-day-men and Defenders were made friends, and joining in sworn brotherhood, became United Irishmen.

At a later period, Henry Joy M'Cracken advised and assisted in the special organization of a body of seven thousand men, originally of the Defenders, to act as a forlorn hope, in case of necessity, out of the twenty-one thousand that were returned fighting men in the County of Antrim; they were directed by a committee, by whom their chief was chosen, who communicated with the committee by a deputy.

In Ulster, the population holding on by small patches of the soil, the influence of agricultural wealth, had the greater number of roots, and that influence ran through every channel of rural society, and likewise through the commercial and manu-facturing classes; the pulpit and the bench there were under aristocratic influence. Nor was the jury-box exempted from it, so that the men who attempted to stem the torrent of corruption in Ulster, had still the heaviest task. The southern mass, consisting of landlords, tenants, churchlords, and labourers, had but four interests, diverging from that which was general; while in Ulster, manufacture and commerce, fictitious capital, fictitious credit, fictitious titles to consideration, presented the numberless interests of the few, in opposition to the one interest of the many.

Such were the difficulties with which the men of Ulster had to contend, besides that perplexity arising from a pensioned clergy, puzzling its followers, with speculations above human comprehension, and instigating them to hate each other, for conscience sake, under the mask of religion.

So complete was the concentration of aristocratic monetary influence, that nothing but its own corruption could destroy it. I remember when power was law, and physical force settled every question. The destruction of the *Northern Star* silenced moral force for a time, and physical force was then resorted to, by the people, for the preservation of life and liberty.

In the battle of the press, Neilson, in the hour of danger, stood alone, as M'Cracken did in the field, at the close of the struggle; all their former auxiliaries having abandoned them in the time of peril. Mr Neilson's partners in the *Northern Star* establishment retired from it when the capital of the concern was consumed by legal tyranny; he continued the struggle of moral force at his own expense; while a prisoner in Kilmainham, the unlawful destruction of his property, by a military mob, took place. Let posterity observe, the providential turn of affairs, how the sword, that was drawn to put down moral force, now rusts in the scabbard by the operation of other powers, admonishing mankind to ascribe the retribution of evil to the true cause, as in the case of *Herod*, who was consumed by worms, for rottenness itself became the proper punishment of that man's exalted wickedness. Moral force, in its operation, resembles that of Herod's visitation; it ultimately works on the opponents of truth like a consuming work.

The *Northern Star* represented the moral force of *Ulster*, sowed the seeds of truth over the land, and the opposition of the enemy only caused its roots to strike deeper in the soil, and they are now springing up in all directions.

Physical force may yet prevail for a time, as we have seen it recently did in China and Afghanistan; but there is music in the sound of moral force, which will be heard like the sound of the cuckoo. The bird lays its eggs, and leaves them for a time; but it will come again and hatch them in due course, and the song will return with the season.

CHAPTER II

I EARLY OBSERVED, that in the different ranks which had sprung up under the influence of war-making wealth, no one rank was willing to throw its interests into the common stock, and act in concert with another for the public benefit. In every rank there were a few honourable exceptions; but these were marked for death, banishment, or for ruin if they had property, wherever the power of the enemy could reach, or bring pretended friends to desert or betray them.

The demands of the popular leaders of that day, were, for a bill to regulate places, one to regulate pensions, and one to make the servants of the crown more responsible. Had Grattan produced drafts of these bills, instead of that of the insurrection bill, by which he pointed out to ministers, at a later period, how to tie the people's hands, he might have done a little good. But Grattan was with a party, not with the people, though he took the test of the United Irishmen from Mr Samuel Neilson, and the rules of the society from its founder. The knowledge he gained is displayed in the bills which originated with him, when he declared in Parliament, that Ireland required a strong government; for a French party existed in the country. The wounds he had inflicted on faction with his tongue, he healed with his pen, when he drew the gagging bills for his country, and thereby made his peace with the high priests and ministers of despotic power; but it is hard for me to note the recollections of fifty-seven years without digression, or be correct in dates. I must only follow my recollection as matters strike me.

Grattan declared, in the House of Commons, that they might as well stamp on the earth to prevent the rising of the

sun, as think to prevent the eventual parliamentary independence of Ireland, when he saw their drift was a Legislative
Union, which, he said, would terminate in a total and perpetual
separation after two civil wars. How far he contributed to their
success in the first civil war, it is difficult to say. The conduct
of public men, of popular men in those times, convinced me,
that so long as men of rank and fortune lead a people, they will
modify abuses, reform to a certain extent, but they never will
remove any real grievances that press down the people.

It was either in the year 1790 or 1791, that the Belfast
Battalion of Volunteers, with the sovereign, Stewart Banks, at
their head, first celebrated the taking of the Bastille, on the
14th of July, and next year a review of the volunteers took
place for the same purpose: the company to which I belonged,
marched into the field in coloured clothes, with green cockades.
We had a green flag, bearing for a motto, on one side— 'Our
Gallic brother was born July 14, 1789. Alas! we are still in
embryo;' and on the other side—'Superstitious galaxy'; 'The
Irish Bastille—let us unite to destroy it.' These are the words,
though somewhat varied by a writer of a history of Belfast; and
I have a better right to know them, being the one who dictated
them, and my brother-in-law, Luke Mullan, painted them on
the flag.

Mr Neilson's incarceration, and the destruction of his printing
materials, left the venal press in quiet possession of the
agricultural interest, which had not then emerged from the
cupidity of former ages, when every man looked into his
neighbour's field, and wished he could annex it to his own. The
higher classes of the old volunteer officers abandoned their
corps, and began to yawn for rank in a mercenary militia.

There are circumstances which should be kept always before
one connected with the events of 1798; to which their production
is mainly to be attributed. As a people, we were excluded from
any share in framing the laws by which we were governed. The
higher ranks (in which there never was, nor never will be a
majority of honest-principled men) usurped the exclusive
exercise of that privilege, as well as many other rights, by
force, fraud, and fiction. By force the poor were subdued, and
dispossessed of their interests in the soil; by fiction the titles of
the spoilers were established; and by fraud on the productive
industry of future generations, the usurpation was continued.

A person called Atkinson, who lived in Belfast, and a Low
Church clergyman near Lisburn (Philip Johnson), organized a

faction of intolerant turbulent men into lodges, like Freemasons, called the Loyal Orange Institution. It at first consisted of persecuting yeomen, renegade 'croppies,' the hangers-on about landlords, and Low Church clergymen; with their spies and informers, all over the country—the bullies of certain houses in garrison towns, and those of fairs and markets in the rural districts. This association, under the nursing care of the magistrates, left no visible protection for either life or property out of its own circle, and its members boasted, that the government protected its institution, and that a judge did not ride the circuit that was not a friend to Orangeism. Their July rites were duly observed by the sacrifice of numerous victims to the memory of King William the Third; and when legal redress was resorted to by the relations and friends of the sufferers, the conduct of the authorities fully justified the above assertion. The character of the Orange lodges was such, that no man who had any regard for his character would appear in them; but most of the United Irishmen, known as the Foreign-aid men, found some means of secret connection with them; some took the Orange oath in personal confidence, and were reported in the lodges to be loyal men.

These renegades were the cause of more bloodshed in 1798, than the open enemy whom we knew and might avoid. Some of the sufferers took personal vengeance, but paid dearly for it, either by death or banishment, and several suffered for acts of which they were known to be innocent; for at that time, there was any money got for swearing; and in every district there were some men, who by taking contradictory oaths, became habituated to swear whatever any cause required, in which they were embarked; and although these were few in proportion to the mass, they were sufficient for the reign of terror, and there were still men of high rank among them, who had the address to retain the confidence of the people, who are ever ready to give such men credit for more than they deserve.

Ulster was the seat of politics, in which there were three parties: those whose industry produced the necessaries of life, those who circulated them, and those whose subsistence depended on fictitious claims and capital, and lived and acted as if men and cattle were created solely for their use and benefit, and to whom a sycophantic clergy were ever ready to bow with the most profound respect. The town of Belfast was the centre of this factitious system, and, with few exceptions, the most corrupt spot on the face of the earth. In Belfast, the

British ministry had, and long continued to have, its sheet anchor, whenever a political storm menaced its interests. These circumstances, and changes in the currency, the staple manufacture of the country, and condition of the people, tended to a state of things, in which hucksters became merchants, merchants became bankers, and bankers became provincial bashaws; and then, as now (1843), when the fitness and capability of Ireland for independence were discussed, the above classes were always with the government. I remember being present at one of these discussions. Mr Henry Joy M'Cracken was the only man present who supposed self dependence possible. His arguments had little effect on the company. One—the chief difficulty with those who opposed his opinion— was, in reference to naval protection. I said, that Ireland was the eye of Europe—it required no naval protection; it was the connecting link in the chain of the commerce of the two hemispheres. When we parted, M'Cracken blamed my rashness, and bade me never use such language while Ireland remained as she then was; 'for' said he, 'there are many mercantile men, and some of them were in that very company, who are efficient members of our society, and who, rather than see their shipping interests or commercial establishments, on the east and northeast of this island, lessened in value, by the increased traffic on the western coast, would see the whole island, and every vestige of our liberty, sunk into the sea.' 'Well,' said I, 'Harry, these are the men that will put the rope on your neck and mine, if ever they get us into their power.' 'Are you afraid of being hanged, Jemmy—' said he. 'It would ill become one, who has pledged his life to his country, to shrink from death in any shape,' I replied; 'but, I confess, I have no desire for that distinction.' 'For my part,' said he, 'I do not desire to die of sickness.'

The struggle at that period, as at the present, was merely between commercial and aristocratical interests, to determine which should have the people as its property, or as its prey; each contending for the greatest share. When an appeal was made to the mass, the mercantile interest had the support of opinion, but the aristocracy, which carried with it the landed interest and the court, had the absolute sway. Grattan was the darling of the merchants, for his exertion in 1782, and Castlereagh that of the landlords; and with these competitors for power—to a certain extent having one common object, the promotion of the interests of the wealthy classes—Pitt rode roughshod over the people, and eventually secured or banished all the active leaders of the north, taking care that a traitor or two, should keep them company in prison or in exile, who might furnish him with their secrets the more easily, having gained their victim's confidence, from having apparently shared his punishment.

The influence of the union* soon began to be felt at all public places, fairs, markets, and social meetings, extending to all the counties of Ulster, for no man of an enlightened mind had intercourse with Belfast, who did not return home determined on disseminating the principles of the union among his neighbours. Strife and quarrelling ceased in all public places, and even intoxication.

The 'Break-of-day boys,' and 'Defenders,' lamented their past indiscretions on both sides, and tracing them to their legitimate source, resolved to avoid the causes which led to them. In short, for a little time, Ulster seemed one united family, the members of which lived together in harmony and peace. A secret delegation to Dublin was resolved on, and I was one of two persons, who were appointed to proceed there, to disseminate our views among the working classes. We succeeded to our wishes, and likewise formed connections with Meath and Kildare, which soon extended to the other counties. In Leinster the gentlemen soon found the people prepared to support them in any effort, and the power of a united population became perceptible everywhere. Our enemies trembled at the prospect of unanimity, they insinuated themselves among the people, and even some of them joined the association. These were the parties who were mainly instrumental in deluding the people into conspiracy, and a desire for foreign aid, pointing out France as the then arbitrator of the destinies of Europe, which the success of her arms seemed to indicate. The people were advised to prepare for action; in 1797 some of their friends who had fled to the Continent were accompanied by traitors, who by the assistance of other traitors at home, deceived the principal leaders *abroad*, and urged them ultimately to consent to attempt with a handful of men, what in reality they knew would have required a considerable and well provided force.

The idea of foreign aid, and French connection, which although the original projectors of the society did not approve

*United Irishmen.

of, was now introduced by men of weight and influence in the societies. Henry Joy M'Cracken was the first who observed the design and operation of this underplot. The majority of the leaders became foreign aid men, and were easily elevated or depressed by the news from France, and amongst their ranks, spies were chiefly found. They were also the prolific source of contradictory rumours, to distract the societies and paralyse confidence.

The appearance of a French fleet in Bantry Bay, brought the rich farmers and shopkeepers into the societies, and with them, all the corruption essential to the objects of the British Ministry, to foster rebellion, to possess the power of subduing it, and to carry a Legislative Union. The new adherents alleged, as a reason for their former reserve, that they thought the societies, only a combination of the poor to get the property of the rich. The societies as a mark of satisfaction at their conversion, and a demonstration of confidence in their wealthy associates, the future leaders, civil and military, were chiefly chosen from their ranks. We had traitors in our camp from the beginning to close of the career of our society. For years our agent in Hamburg (Mr Turner), and one of our state prisoners, at Fort George, were furnishing Pitt with all our secrets, foreign and domestic. M'Cracken, who was by far the most deserving of all our northern leaders, observed that what we had latterly gained in numbers, we lost in worth: he foresaw that the corruption of Ulster would endanger the union in the south. Agents had been sent to Paris at an early period of the revolution, and while the Republican party predominated, funds were at their disposal, but on the change of parties in France, and the unfavourable turn of affairs at home, many of the refugees were left to starve, or to embarrass private friends. Such was the state of the refugees, when those from Fort George arrived in Paris. For the reason above stated Bonaparte did not like the Irish, and for the same reason they had no confidence in him. It was easy to persuade them, that he was in treaty with the British Government to banish them from France; and even in America, their asylum had been doubtful under one president. But the republican spirit of the Irish refugees did not accord with Bonaparte's imperial views, this was the chief cause of his unfavourable dispositions towards them. The first attempt at invasion, that of Hoche's expedition, seemed powerful enough, but was disconcerted by separation from their commander at an unfavourable season. The aristocrats rushed into the societies, complaining that they had only been deterred from joining, from a suspicion that foreign aid could not be had, but that they now most earnestly wished to join in every prudent attempt to free their country.

Their plausible pretensions soon lulled the people into confidence, and having obtained it, they began to persuade the people that if the French came here with a formidable force they would hold the country as conquered, that a few experienced officers, an able general, and a small supply of arms and ammunition, was all that would be required; and that the standard once raised would soon collect a sufficient force.

This being communicated to Bartholomew Teeling, in Paris, he made the demand of the French Government, which they reluctantly complied with, as afterwards became evident from their ordering him immediately to the place of embarkation, and then delaying the sailing of the expedition, by retaining the pay of the troops, until General Humbert had to force the officer whose duty it was, to pay the troops, which he said he only delayed for want of orders.

The other half of the expedition, with J. N. Tandy, was detained until the defeat of the first was known at Paris, and from this it is conjectured, if not fully ascertained, that there was treachery all along with the French Government, for Admiral Sir John Borlace Warren, knew when to fall in with the last division of their fleet, with a superior force, and to capture it in sight of land.

General Hoche, who commanded the expedition to Bantry Bay, was of opinion that the frigate in which he sailed was separated from the rest of the fleet by treachery, and this is thought by all who knew him, to have broken his heart, as he died soon after.

The internal enemies of Ireland were no less successful at home than abroad, headed and directed by a renegade volunteer, Castlereagh, whose very name rouses all the angry passions of the Irish heart.

The secret of organization of the people, while it sheltered treachery and nourished spies, completely tied the hands of the honest and resolute: this class, naturally unsuspecting, and possessing moral, as well as military, courage, patiently waited the signal for action, from the year 1797, until May, 1798, whilst the country, suffering every species of military depredation, was driven to distraction.

The counties of Wexford and Wicklow, which had not been

so long organized, were selected by government for singular vengeance. A considerable number of the Foundling Hospital Boys, of Dublin, had been nursed in those counties, and having settled in it, without any natural ties of blood or kindred, prejudiced by their education against the Roman Catholics they were found to be ready tools, from their local knowledge, to point out the men who were suspected. Thus they became a public scourge in those parts: the corrupt and the corruptible, of every circle, from the Giant's Causeway to Cape Clear, were known to the dominant despotism of that day, and regularly employed either as yeomen or spies.

The seeds of corruption, it was evident to me, were sown in our society, but I was unable to convince my acquaintances, my observation was only useful to myself, and prepared me for the worst, which realized my dreariest forebodings, without, however, sinking my spirits in the least, or making me regret any step I had taken. Although I executed the part assigned me, in every movement cheerfully, I was always prepared for defeat, for none of our leaders seemed to me perfectly acquainted with the main cause of social derangement, if I except Neilson, M'Cracken, Russell, and Emmet. It was my settled opinion that the condition of the labouring class, was the fundamental question at issue between the rulers and the people, and there could be no solid foundation for liberty, till measures were adopted that went to the root of the evil, and were specially directed to the restoration of the natural right of the people, the right of deriving a subsistence from the soil on which their labour was expended. The plan of the United Irishmen was carried into effect with success, until Lord Castlereagh had the address to get into the confidence of a United Irishman, named James Breese, who afterwards suffered death in '98; by taking the test or oath of the society, he was put in possession of all the secrets of the society that Breese was acquainted with, by which means he could weigh all the other secret informations he received, and find out proper agents for any purpose he might require.

CHAPTER III

IN THE SPRING OF 1796, I was sent to Dublin, with a man named Metcalfe, as delegates from the Belfast Society of United Irishmen, to introduce the system among the operatives in the capital. We were promised assistance in money, which did not arrive, and the men to whom we were recommended, showed no inclination to forward our designs, but rather discouraged us; we had to rely on our own exertions. One of them directed us to a man we might rely on, but took care to send him word not to see us; the man was denied, but afterwards acknowledged that he had seen us through a hole in the door. I had the pleasure of freeing the same man at a later period out of Roscommon goal, by appearing at the assizes as a recruiting sergeant. I took up my residence at Balbriggan, in the character of a silk-weaver from Scotland, and used to come backwards and forwards, between Dublin and that town, without exciting suspicion for some time.

The man with whom I worked in Balbriggan was a bitter Orangeman, and at length I became an object of suspicion to him, on learning which, I returned to Dublin, and succeeded in obtaining my freedom to work in the Liberty, which enabled me to promote the objects of my mission.

From Dublin the Union soon reached the other provinces, and a national committee was formed, which met in Dublin. The leading men were still unknown to the societies, for no one knew anything of the persons belonging to them, besides those who met in his own society, except the delegates who met in baronial committee, and the delegates from it again who met in the county committee, and those from the counties who met in the provincial committee, and appointed a national council, or executive.

After having formed a society, and obtained a deputation to Belfast, I returned to the north, to report, and was again sent to Dublin to complete the organization among the workmen. I got to work on my arrival, and the circle of friends increased; societies were formed through the City and Liberties, and former connections were renewed; but the imprudence of my comrade brought us again under suspicion. He was a Protestant; I a Presbyterian. One of the Dublin societies had entrusted a secret of some importance to him, and there was a breach of confidence on his part. I was brought under suspicion unjustly, and without cause; however, it was thought most prudent to drown us both; for which purpose an appointment was made with us to attend a meeting outside of the Circular-road by the side of the Royal Canal, where six men were appointed to meet, and drown us. We kept the appointment until it grew dark, and returned to our lodging. On going to work next day, I observed my employer change colour when I appeared. I inquired what was the matter: I insisted on his candidly informing me what caused his agitation. The truth came out—I was suspected of having betrayed the secret which my comrade had divulged. I had been denounced—my doom had been pronounced—and the man who had left his home to execute his murderous commission, had been accidentally prevented from carrying it into effect: he had met a comrade on the way to the place of appointment, had accepted an invitation to drink with him, and the time of the appointment expired before he quitted the public house.

Such meditated acts even were injurious to our cause; but it was the object of our enemies to have wretches in our ranks to blacken the character of our society, and to have crimes ascribed to its members. Nay, even to have them committed in their name, of which they were wholly guiltless. They had even highway robberies, and house-breaking offences, committed in our name.

I met a man, named Connell, in Dublin, who said he came from the County of Cavan; he lived at Bluebells, and invited me to breakfast there with him. He introduced me to his family, as a friend to our country from Belfast. He had a stout-looking son, to whom he introduced me; and also six of his comrades, whom he said belonged to a society of United Irishmen. He told me they lived about the commons of Crumlin. A few nights after, the young man and his mother called where I worked, and asked my employer and myself to take a walk. Our road was up the canal, and the old woman kept my employer in talk until the young man and I were out of sight, for it was then dusk. She persuaded him to go home, as she said there would be a meeting at her house, and her husband wanted to introduce me to the neighbours. There was a line of high trees, and a path behind them, and she could pass on unnoticed by us. I wished to stop until the old people would come up, but my companion said he would stop at a lock that was before us. We stopped at the lock, and he began to whistle a tune, when a number of men came out on the road, and he then told me I was on a command. 'What for?' said I, 'To lift some arms,' was his reply; 'and we want your north country tongue to give orders.' I then saw my situation, and asked if there 'was any money in the way?' 'We don't demand it,' said he; 'but if it is offered, we don't refuse it.' 'I have no arms,' said I; 'here is a blunderbuss,' answered one of the company. I took it, drew the ramrod, and found it loaded. 'I'll use no arms but what I load myself,' said I. They gave me a rod, with which I managed to draw the charge; I tried the flint, and put in a heavy charge of swanshot, and, clapping the muzzle to Connell's breast, I said to his comrades—'you cannot save him; if one of you move, he is a dead man; you shall not make me rob. Do you, Connell, walk before me, until I get within a race of the watch; I will not injure you if you obey; turn your back, and walk before me.' He obeyed, and I warned his comrades not to follow us. I made him keep his hands down by his side, for fear he might have pistols; and when I came within a short distance of the watch, I made him stand; I then walked backwards until I could just see him, and, holding up the blunderbuss, flung it into a meadow, and took to my heels.

I thought it advisable to leave Dublin for some time. I returned home to Belfast; but was soon ordered back to Dublin. I was charged with a message to the Kilmainham prisoners. I stopped with them all night; and in the morning I was standing, conversing with Tom Story, in one of the cells, looking into the condemned yard, when I saw Connell crossing the yard, with bolts on him. Storey informed me, that he had been sentenced to death, for a highway robbery, committed by a gang of robbers, called the Crumlin gang, of which he was the chief.

An informer, named Edward John Newell, was procured by

George Murdoch, a hearth-tax collector, near Belfast. Among other services performed by him, he had pointed out the soldiers who were shot at Blaris-camp. Newell had also five young men of Belfast arrested, who had been sent to Dublin for trial at the Four Courts. He was to have appeared as a witness against them, but the trials were put off, for that term, for want of a material witness in their defence; H. J. M'Cracken, who could not attend from bad health. In the meantime, a criminal correspondence was discovered between Newell and Murdoch's wife. The letters which passed between them were sent up from the north, and communicated by me to Murdoch. The consequences were, that the coalition between these worthies, then living in the castle, were broken up. They quarelled, and Murdoch shot at Newell, in the castle-yard, and, for that act, was sent to Newgate, but was only confined a few days; and, on his liberation, Newell fled to the north, taking with him Murdoch's wife. After a trip, in the direction of the Giant's Causeway, he returned to Doagh, and lived there in concealment for some time. At length, when he was about to leave the country, he wrote to Murdoch, telling him where he would find his wife. Newell staid with her at the inn, until Murdoch, and his son Robert, appeared at the door, in a carriage, and then escaped by a back window. What became of him afterwards, little is known; but Murdoch returned with his wife, as if nothing of the kind had ever happened!

If any committee, or body of men, directors, or managers of assassinations, had existed in any part of Ireland, some traces of the proceedings, discussions, or reports, in reference to such an object, would be forthcoming; but nonesuch are in existence, for the best of reasons, because no such committees ever existed. It is the duty of the historian, in handing down the virtues and vices of the age he treats of, as examples to the virtues, and warning to the vicious to make the information he obtains confirmatory of the maxim—'Virtue carries with it its own reward, and vice its punishment.'

In all the societies, or committees, or in any meeting that ever I attended, I never heard a system of assassination advocated. My motion in the 'Baronial Committee, to exclude any man that would advise it, was opposed, on the ground, that the agitation of the question would only extend an idea, that no good man ought to be thought capable of harbouring.

An attempt was made to form a committee to manage assassination, of which it is only necessary to say, *Newell* was one of the agents employed for that purpose, he was seen through by the United Irishmen, and disappointed. We all set our faces against it, and our success is evident; for, if such a system had any existence, evidence of it could easily be had; and no such evidence was ever brought forward on any trial. Assassination was the work of individuals, either in defence of their lives, or that of their associates. Neilson, M'Cracken, and Russell, were altogether adverse to it. It was by their advice that I brought forward the motion in our society, formerly mentioned; and the motion would have been brought forward again, but from the state of the times; the public mind was ill prepared for its calm discussion. Had such a committee been formed in Belfast, it could not have been kept secret, as most of its advocates that I knew, became Orangemen, on our reverse of fortune.

Nicholas Maginn, of Saintfield, the noted informer, and protegee of Lord Castlereagh's spiritual guide and tutor, the Rev. John Cleland, had a meeting in his neighbourhood, to assassinate the Marquis of Downshire; but the Marquis escaped, by taking a different way home from that by which he was expected to pass; which prevented any further collection of assassins in that county. This account I had from the very best authority.

The preceding account was given to me by one of the Northerns, who was as undaunted in the field, as he was worthy of credit and respect—Thomas Hunter, a native of Killinchey. On his deathbed, he was asked, by a woman in attendance on him in his last moments, if he would wish to *turn?* He seemed not to understand the question, or his thoughts were running on events which had been long uppermost in his mind, he replied—'*No; I will never turn, or take a bribe.*' These were nearly his last words. He had stood the brunt of the battles of Saintfield and Ballynahinch.

The following anecdote I had from John Murphy, one of the young men who was arrested with Hart and Weldon, on the evidence of William Lawler, who had caused them to become Defenders, and then had them arrested in 1797. The names of the young men were, John Murphy, John Newburn, John Cusac, John Brady, John O'Leary, Patrick Hart, and a dragoon, named Weldon. Counsellor Curran was employed by Murphy's mother to defend her son. Counsellor M'Nally was employed to defend O'Leary, who was tried and acquitted, on the ground '*that the witness was an atheist*'; upon which admission,

Alderman James led the witness to the quarters of the informers, at the Castle, where he had the sacrament administered to him. Hart and Weldon were convicted: the others were liberated: and some of them became my associates and friends, when I was sent from Belfast to Dublin, to introduce the Union.

O'Leary, subsequently, went to Roscommon, and through his imprudence, was committed to jail there. A young man, named Richard Dry, had been sent from Dublin with money to him, and was committed also. Two other men had been sent, and were taken in Mullingar, and were sent to the Provost, in Dublin. I was sent for the same purpose, from Belfast, with a comrade, named Daniel Digney. We went through the counties of Monaghan, Cavan, Armagh, and Leitrim. We formed a county committee in Castleblany, and societies in the other counties, as we passed. But, arriving at Elfin, the gentleman to whom we were directed, Colonel James Plunket, was in Dublin, and all we could learn of him was, that he was recruiting for some regiment. We returned to Belfast, and were sent to Dublin along with William Putnam M'Cabe, and got beating orders. We had left five hundred copies of our constitution in and near Elfin, and went there for headquarters, to wait the coming assizes.

Our money failed, and I was sent to Dublin, by M'Cabe, for more. The man to whom I was directed, was on his deathbed, and I had to go to Stratford, in the County of Wicklow, to sell a horse that M'Cabe had left with the brother of this person. The horse was sold, but the money was not forthcoming.

I started for Roscommon, in the disguise of a soldier. I took the rank of a serjeant. The assizes had begun. Colonel Plunket was there, and likewise, M'Cabe, in the character of an officer of militia, on recruiting service. I enlisted Dry in the dock; and when he was called to the bar, and represented as a vagabond, the colonel and the pretended captain interfered, and I got my recruit. I would have got O'Leary also, but for his own imprudence. He made such a noise in the dock, with the chains and bolts he had on, that he had been ordered back to his cell, before the arrangements were completed.

M'Cabe, Dry, and myself, went to Strokestown, settled our accounts, and started for Athlone, where we parted—M'Cabe for Dublin, and I for Cashcarrigan, in the County Leitrim, to join my comrade, and return to Belfast. Dry proceeded to Cork, and there had the misfortune to be recognized by an Antrim militia man, named M'Dermot, who prosecuted him, and transported him to Botany Bay. O'Leary was left in prison, through his own imprudence, and I never heard of his liberation.

Having assisted in forming the County Monaghan committee, in Castleblany, on a market day, when several very respectable linen merchants were there, we planted the Union at Maguire's-bridge, Clones, Enniskillen, Ballynamore, Cashcarrigan, Carrick-on-Shannon and Strokestown, where we saw delegates from a body of the old Defenders, and initiated them. We left five hundred copies of the constitution in Roscommon, and on our return home, formed committees in Ballyhays, Butler's-bridge, and Newtown Hamilton. Such of these connections as we were able to visit the second time, were increasing rapidly.

The substance of the reports, however, which we were obliged to deliver in, was communicated to the county committee, of which Maginn, the informer, was a member; and likewise to the Mudler's Society of which Hughes was a member. No real secrecy ever existed among us; for as soon as any efficient measure was proposed, the government was instantly prepared, if not to prevent its execution, yet eventually to counteract its effects.

The progress of the revolution in France had excited the mass of the people in this country, and had put the aristocrats to their shifts. The people, as appeared afterwards, wished to rise at various times, trusting solely to their own resources; but were always withheld by their committees, who were, for the most part, aristocrats, and foreign-aid men, who contrived to involve the people with France, thereby frightening government, and enhancing their own value as traitors. Many of them thus obtained and enjoyed tolerable advantages, and some hold them, even unto this day.

Mr Samuel Turner, of Newry, had made great professions of patriotism at an early period. On one occasion, he walked into an inn, in Newry, and was there met by Lord Carhampton, who, seeing a green handkerchief on his neck, proceeded, very quietly, to take it off. Turner sent Carhampton a challenge, and the act served as an apology for him to fly, for fear of arrest. He fled, and settled in Hamburg, where he was entrusted, by the executive, with carrying on the correspondence between the Irish and French executives, always taking care to furnish Pitt with true copies of the correspondence.

Another informer, named H——, formerly a shipbroker of Belfast, was one of the prisoners in Fort George. A coolness had been occasioned among them, from a conversation between

Robert Simms and Arthur O'Connor, in which they agreed, that the then present constitution of France, was too good for Ireland. This idea was resented by Joseph Cuthbert, and some others, and occasioned very warm words—Cuthbert asserting, that no constitution could be too good for Ireland. 'I am talking to a politician, not to you, Joe,' said O'Connor. Joe, and his friends, took that ill. Russell took no part in the debate, but was not of O'Connor's or of Simms' opinion.

Prior to this, some attempt had been made by individuals, to open a communication with the Scotch militia, and H——, having had a knowledge of it, wrote to Pitt about it, who, being in communication with Turner, did not answer H——'s letter; and the prisoners having notice of an expedition preparing in the Scheldt, were cheered by that prospect, although the misunderstanding still continued individually among them. One night, as they were in society over a glass of punch, H——, observing a feeling of distrust prevailed against him, which he could not account for, concluded that his letters had been intercepted, and in a moment of compunction, of fear or of unguarded conduct, he made a confession with tears and protestations, that he would never follow up his information. Peace coming on, the discharge or banishment of the state prisoners ensued. Messrs H—— and Turner were permitted to return.

Mr John Palmer, of Cutpurse-row, formerly eminent in the hosiery line, and a sincere friend of our cause, had a son named John, one of the warmest and most faithful friends I ever had. He and William Putnam M'Cabe, met Major Sirr and his party in Bridgfoot Street, on their way to arrest Lord Edward Fitzgerald. The major stopped them, and M'Cabe knocked him down, and Palmer made a stab at the major's neck, which cut through his neck handkerchief. *Palmer would have succeeded in his attack, but M'Cabe prevented him.* M'Cabe was arrested the same night, Palmer was arrested two days subsequently; but in the bustle about the capture of Lord Edward, before the major had time to visit the persons sent to prison, Miss Biddy Palmer, sister to the young man, went to the castle, and, meeting Major Sirr, she hung on him, and would not let him go until he gave her an order for her brother's liberation, not knowing that he was the man who wounded him the night before.

M'Cabe, no less fortunate, through being familiar with the Scotch dialect, and the gaol being under a Highland guard, he passed on a Highland sergeant for the son of a manufacturer in Glasgow, named Brand. The sergeant went to his officer, and, as no complaint lay against him, he was liberated. But when the major came to Newgate a few hours after, a rigorous pursuit was commenced after both Palmer and M'Cabe. Palmer immediately fled to France, and from thence to Holland. He had learned that one Bureand, who had formerly been a spy in Ireland, was employed in the same branch of business in Holland. Although this man had run away from the Castle of Dublin, and written against government, Palmer set off on foot, with the design of frustrating this man's villany, and travelled from Paris to Hamburg, and mostly barefooted, where he met Samuel Turner, and entered freely into communication with him. Palmer gave him a gold watch to keep for him, lest distress might force him to sell it, the watch having belonged to his mother, who was dead. His father had sent him thirty guineas by a man named Murky, which he never got. However, under every disadvantage, he had Bureand arrested, and put into the hands of the French authorities. But Bureand's employers exerted their influence, and caused him soon to be released; while Palmer was forced by want to enlist in a Dutch regiment, and, while bathing with some recruits in the Scheldt, was drowned. Rumour attributed his death to Bureand's vindictive feelings.

When Turner returned to Dublin, and was applied to for the watch by his sister, then Mrs Horan, he coolly replied, 'he did recollect something of a watch he got from her brother, but forgot what became of it.'

At Cashcarragan, we learned that a man named Toby Peter, had seen us there as we passed that way before, and that a chapel in the neighbourhood had been searched for us, the Sunday before. We went over the Cash to one Dignum, a school-master, who saw us safe on the Ballyanmore road, before day-break next morning.

We had formed some acquaintance in Ballynamore, but we changed our route, and came through Belturbet to Butler's-bridge, in the County Cavan, and from thence proceeded to Newry. My comrade, being then among his relations and friends, stopped there for some time, but came with me as far as the old four-mile house, kept by Andrew Stewart; we went into a room, where six of the City Limerick Militia sat refreshing themselves, being on a march to Carrickfergus, for one of their men had been committed to gaol, on the oath of a woman, charging him with a rape, of which they said he was innocent, being taken for another man, which they were prepared to prove. As I was for Belfast, I joined their company; and while we were talking, we heard a scream. As I sat next the door, I sprang into the hall, and the first thing I saw was a horseman riding into the door, with his sword drawn, and a woman, with a child in her arms, creeping under the stairs, at the end of the hall. I had a sword in my hand—I drew the sword, and the horseman, not having room enough to use his sabre, it struck against the ceiling, when he attempted to cut at me; I threatened to run him through, if he did not instantly leave. By this time the soldiers turned out, and drew their bayonets. The horseman, on retiring, ran his horse's heels against a door in the hall, and broke it; we followed him out, and saw another, they both rode slowly on towards Banbridge. The affrighted woman then told us, that two of the same corps had stopped at the door just before they came up, called each for a tumbler of beer, drank it, and threw the tumblers on the flags at the door, and rode off, without paying anything; that, on account of her standing at the door, and looking after them, she thought it caused the others, who had just come in sight, to behave as they had done. While we were at the door, the main body came up, with an officer at their head, whose name, we were told, was Wardle.

A Limerick soldier, named Maher, demanded of the officer if he had given orders for the 'raking' of the house. The officer said, 'who are you, sir?' Maher replied, 'I am a soldier of the City Limerick Militia.' 'Where is your officer?' demanded the English officer. 'I command this party,' said Maher, 'and, being here to refresh, and seeing the house perfectly orderly, I think it my duty to acquaint your honour with the circumstance.' The officer ordered a party forthwith to dismount the two soldiers of his party, and march them away on foot; and desired Stewart to make out his bill of the damage, and come into Banbridge, and it should be paid. But Stewart said he knew where he lived, and might injure him again, and he refused to do so. I went with the Limerick men into Banbridge, and being, as they thought, in the recruiting service, they got me a billet for two men, which I did not think right to use; but after spending the evening with them, I went to a lodging-house where some of the aforesaid horsemen (the Ancient Britons) were billeted. I slept but little, and the next day proceeded on my journey to Belfast, and was glad to get home, having travelled—

	MILES
To Roscommon, and home to Belfast	200
To Dublin	80
To Prosperous, and back to Dublin	30
To Roscommon from Dublin	79
To Dublin from Roscommon	79
To Stratford on Slaney from Dublin	26
To Dublin from Stratford	26
Astray in the Mountains of Wicklow	8
From Dublin to Roscommon	79
From Roscommon to Belfast, by Athlone	100
	707

Early in 1797, we had been led to expect a movement; but what prevented it I know no more of, than what I was told by William Putnam M'Cabe. He said he had travelled from Dublin with Colonel James Plunket, of Elfin, and another gentleman, a school-fellow of Bonaparte, who had been a soldier, by profession, on the Continent (whether in the French or German service I do not know), and John Hughes of Belfast, who turned informer in 1798, but was at that time one of Lord Edward's confidential acquaintances, which confidence continued until the very day of Lord Edward's arrest. After viewing the camp at Blaris and the adjacent country, the gentleman said, that if the people were firm, and would stand to each other, the conquest of the camp and country would be easy— the counties of Antrim and Down had only so to be directed, to act in concert to cut off the communication with the camp—to secure some guns that were then in Hillsborough, with the view of using double-headed shot against the wooden houses that were in the vicinity of the camp, and which would render it impossible for the troops to remain there. To ascertain if the organization was as complete as it was reported, the gentlemen went over the mountain to Crumlin, and stopped at John Dickey's house. His brother James, who suffered in 1798, called a meeting of his company after night-fall, that the gentlemen might see them; but when the men were assembled, and the gentlemen ready to inspect them, James Dickey ran to them with an alarm, that the army were coming to disperse or apprehend them; and they, not knowing why they had been called together, dispersed at once and were represented by James Dickey as cowards; and when the gentlemen returned to Hillsborough next day, they learned that the guns had been just removed to the camp. They then went back to Dublin, disappointed, and reported that the north was not in a condition to act. Of this I was not an eyewitness, having had the report, as I give it, from Wm Putnam M'Cabe, who said he was present. It was soon felt in the societies that some disappointment had taken place, and it began to be whispered that our leaders had refused to act.

Plunkett still continued in confidence, and accepted the command of the County Roscommon; but when the French landed at Killala, he surrendered, and was permitted to go to England. He was a man in whom I was deceived, for, when in his company, he appeared to be a person whose fidelity to our cause was not to be questioned.

In looking back at the conduct of such men as Plunkett, of which we had many such in the association, I do not rank them with the common herd of traitors, they were rather men who unthinkingly staked more than was really in them—they were like paper money, current for the time, keeping business afloat without any intrinsic value.

CHAPTER IV

THE ORGANIZATION of the north being completed, the leaders, civil and military, chosen from the middle ranks, were exposed to greater danger from traitors, than labourers or tradesmen.

The desire of distinction was a motive that induced many to accept of appointments, without seeing the responsibility attached to them, or the consequence to others of their delinquency, which led them to save themselves at any price, even the blood of the men who appointed them.

The men of this last sort, were so mixed with the masses, that the derangement of our plans was an easy task to the traitors. Russell, the first appointed general of Down, was a prisoner at Kilmainham. The Rev. Steele Dixon was appointed in his stead. The general of Antrim was arrested with Russell, but was liberated, and had gone home when the tortures commenced. It was agreed between him and another chief, who was to lead a forlorn hope, in case of necessity, that I should attend either as aide-de-camp.

The general of Antrim either misunderstood, or knowingly and wilfully misrepresented, the signal for rising on the 21st of May, and kept us in suspense until the beginning of June. Blood had been shed in the south, and the people of the north became impatient. I went to the general of Antrim and told him that an irregular movement could not long be prevented. He said he would certainly call them out; I went among the people and told them what he said; they wanted to know who he was; I said, they would know that when he appeared, not being at liberty to tell his name, which traitors afterwards made a charge against me. The general summoned me, and sent me on a command to the south, and said he had called a meeting of his colonels that day. I was met on my way by Henry J. M'Cracken, who stopped me, and said the general had not obeyed the signal for general action, and must be watched. I went home by his orders, and that evening he came to my house, we learned that the general had resigned; and John Hughes, the informer, being the medium of communication between Down and Antrim, he sent me with a letter to Dr Dixon, but he had been arrested that day. Hughes sent me subsequently to different places to look for him, but he knew well my labour was lost.

The organization of the north being thus deranged, the colonels flinched, and the chief of the Antrim men, the forlorn hope party of the union, not appearing, the duty fell on Henry J. M'Cracken; he sent fighting orders to the colonels of Antrim, three of whom sent the identical orders to General Nugent [the British Commander] and the messenger he sent to Down proving unfaithful, the people of Down had no correct knowledge of affairs at Antrim, until they heard of the battle of the 7th of June.

The greatest part of our officers, especially of those who were called colonels, either gave secret information to the enemy, or neutralized the exertions of individuals as far as their influence extended.

I never knew a single colonel in the County of Antrim, who, when the time for active measures came, had drawn out his men, or commanded them, in that character. They had, however, a sufficient apology, for the general-in-chief whom they had appointed, resigned on the eve of action.

We were thus situated, forced by burning of houses, and the torturing of the peasantry, into resistance. Without the due appointment of superior officers in the place of those who had resigned and abandoned the cause.

I have already given you some account of the battle of Antrim [see Chapter VIII]; on some points, and not unimportant ones, you were misinformed by the Rev. Mr M'Cartney [a magistrate]. I was present on that occasion, and not a mere spectator of that battle. I pointed out to you, on the spot, the ground we occupied, and the several places where our people, at the onset, had triumphantly charged their enemies, and had been at last repulsed by them. Previous to our march for Antrim I was not appointed to any command; I had refused to accept of any. In the front rank there were eighteen men, most of them personal friends and acquaintances of my own, led by a man named John M'Gladdery. I was in that front rank; and it was allowed by our opponents the men belonging to it marched up the main street, and met the enemies troops in good order, and did the duty assigned to them in a becoming manner. The first position taken was the church-yard, which commands the main street. There our green banner was unfurled, and M'Cracken was stationed with his principal officers about him.

When the street firing on us commenced, a girl came up to us, in the church-yard, and told our leader there was a loop-hole in the wall where he had better go. She had come there in the midst of the firing to point it out to him. When the panic occurred, and the party in reserve mistook the flight of some dragoons for a charge on their companions, M'Cracken on quitting the church-yard to check the disorder, left me in command of that place, and I maintained it as long as there was a hope of keeping possession of the town.

I wish to correct a few errors in the statement of Dr Macartney's, respecting the battle of Antrim. It is not true, that we had two pieces of cannon at Antrim, we had a brass piece which had belonged to the Volunteers. It, and another of the same description, had been buried without the knowledge of the Rev. Mr Campbell, in his Meeting House at Templepatrick. When the Monaghan Militia were burning the village of Temple-patrick, the other piece was discovered, and Mr Campbell, who knew nothing whatsoever of the concealment of the pieces there, was suspected to have had a guilty knowledge of the fact, and was never forgiven by Lord Templeton. The men who were in the foremost ranks of the people, marching into Antrim, were a small body of the Roughforth Volunteers, remarkably steady men, they came on in three files, six deep. The column that followed consisted of Templepatrick and Carmoney men, and some of the Killead people, who had arms. Those of the Campbell family were particularly distinguished among them for their courage; Joshua and Henry fell in the action.

It is stated by Mr Macartney, that the people marched to music, or that the air of the 'Lass of Richmond Hill' was played. We had no musical instruments of any kind amongst us. A man of the name of Harvey commenced singing 'The Marseillaise Hymn,' as we marched into the town, in which his companions joined, but thinking we needed a more lively air, I struck up a verse of a merry Irish song, which was soon joined in by our party.

With respect to persons dressed in green uniform amongst us, the only green uniform at the battle of Antrim was worn by Robert Wilson, which uniform I had succeeded in bringing out of Belfast, in a sack the day that the flogging of the people commenced there. Wilson was a young man of great courage, and excellent conduct and discretion. He had been very active all along, and always behaved with prudence and resolution. His family were highly respectable, his father held a situation in the Belfast Bank.

Mr Macartney, and the yeomen he commanded, after the burning of some houses in the town, had taken refuge behind the wall of the park of Lord Massarene, in front of the high street, and occasionally rose up and fired some shots down the street. Close to the market-house, near the castle gate, some yeomen and horse soldiers kept their ground, the yeomen had two pieces of cannon there, which were soon silenced. We were about to attack the horsemen when a body of Ballyclare men entered the town by the west-end street, and by Bow Lane. This caused some confusion, and the troops at the market-house profitted by it to renew their fire, and took off some of our leaders. The people began to give way, and in attempting to stop the fugitives, M'Cracken, who proceeding with a party of men, by the rear of the houses, to dislodge the yeomen stationed in Lord Massarene's park, was borne down, disobeyed, and deserted by the panic struck multitude. He then made his way to Donogore Hill, along with Robert Wilson, where he expected to find a body of men in reserve, but all his plans had been frustrated by the defection of the military chiefs. James Agnew Farrel, and Mr Quin, a person employed in the salt works at Larne, had been appointed colonels, but neither acted. Farrel either brought, or sent, his fighting orders to General Nugent, and then he went to Scotland. One of our prisoners was a Captain George Mason M'Claverty, who had been taken that morning in his house, and carried to Donegal Hill. He used every argument to prevail on the people to disperse and return to their homes, promising them every protection in his power. He subsequently fulfilled his promise to the letter, not one of the persons in his neighbourhood, many of whom he had seen in arms that day, did he suffer to be troubled or prosecuted. He was one of the most humane and just magistrates in the county. The number of the people killed in the town, that is to say in the action, was very few. James M'Glathery, who had a command, wrote a sketch of the action, which Miss M'Cracken saw in the hands of his sister, Mrs Shaw, of Belfast, in which it was stated that only five or six of the people were killed in the town in action and H. J. M'Cracken said the statement was correct. The dead bodies of both parties were buried in the sands, at Shane's Castle, but those of the people, who were found slain in the fields, were buried in the crossroads at Muckamore, where it had been customary to inter those who committed suicide.

While any prospect of serving our cause appeared to exist, a few of us remained in arms; our ranks at length diminished, the influence of the merchants on the manufacturers, and that of the manufacturers on the workmen, formed a strong claim of pecuniary interests in the province of *Ulster*, so that shelter or relief of any kind afforded to those who stood out, was at the risk of the life and property of the giver.

The very perfection of our organization in *Ulster* gave treachery the greater scope, from the greater intercourse it caused in societies and committees, and numbers of persons, thus becoming personally known to each other, the organization of treachery was rendered still more complete, and, if a comparative few had not thrown their lives into the scale, Castlereagh's plan of keeping the north and south divided, must have sooner succeeded.

When all our leaders deserted us, Henry Joy M'Cracken stood alone faithful to the last. He led on the forlorn hope of the cause at Antrim, and brought the government to terms with all but the leaders.

He died, rather than prove a traitor to his cause, of which fact I am still a living witness, who shared in all his exertions while he lived, and defy any authentic contradiction of that assertion now, or at any future date.

On the 7th of June, 1798, the Braid men had assembled near Broughshane, and marched for Ballymena. They were met, on the way, by some yeomen from Ballymena, whom they took prisoners, and marched back to town. The prisoners seeing their neighbours were suffered to carry their arms, until they should deposit them in the market-house, but when they were on the stairs, going up to the market-house, one of the prisoners, named Davison, having a blunderbuss, discharged it at the people, killed one man, and wounded another, firing then commenced from both parties, several fell in the streets, and the yeomen got in safely into the house. The people left the street for some little time, until a tar barrel was set on fire under the ceiling, and some shots were fired up through it, one of which killed a yeoman; the smoke of the burning tar, admonished the yeomen of their danger, they threw out their arms, and begged for mercy, which was granted, and they were put into the Black-hole under the market-house. A jury sat on the man who broke the peace, and he was condemned to die: two imprudent young men went to put the sentence into immediate execution, and were followed by others, but, on entering the cell, they found the man they were in search of, sitting on some timber that lay there. They ordered him to rise, he refused, and one of them struck him with the butt of his musket, he fell back over the timber on which he sat, and one of the young men taking him by the hand, to raise him on his feet, having a dagger in the other, the yeoman seized the weapon, and drove it through the young man's breast bone, who exclaimed 'I am killed.' Another young man then rushed forward and received three wounds, when an old man entered took hold of the prisoner, and though he was wounded by the yeoman in nine places, the old man dragged him to the door, and there he died by the pike. The other wounded man recovered, but the old man was afterwards prosecuted, and suffered death in Ballymena.

The people continued to flock into Ballymena for two days; but treachery was too well organized in the middle ranks, particularly among the rich farmers, who discouraged their neighbours with contradictory reports.

An officer of the Volunteers of 1784, had the command of the town of Ballymena at this time. He said he had 11,000 men under his command, with whom he would march for Dublin; that he would put the Kells men in the advanced guard, to prevent them from running home again. We obeyed his order; joined the Kells-men, who were ordered to Donegore-hill, and on our march were followed by a young man on horseback, who reported, as he rode along our lines, that peace had been made; that Lord O'Neil had forgiven all his tenants a year's rent, and they had returned home; and that the men at Toombridge had accepted the terms, and dispersed, which news produced a mutiny. We then returned to Kells—this was on the 9th—and on the 10th, in the morning, we learned that the leaders in Ballymena had deserted and the people had dispersed; the Kells-men followed the example. Mr M'Cracken had been employed in collecting a few stragglers in the mountains, mostly Belfast-men, who could not go home; and such as were willing to continue in arms marched with him.

On Saturday, the 9th of June, I joined the Kells-men, and was told that there were some boxes of new arms in the neighbourhood, that would be distributed as soon as required. I got a fine-looking new musket, which my comrade fancied, and I gave it to him. He brought it to Themish before he discovered that the touch-hole was only bored sufficiently far into the barrel to prevent discovery, without its being tried by a pin; my comrade threw it on the green. Whether his doing so prevented us from getting more new arms or not, I do not know; but we saw but the one musket. The open danger which we ran, was nothing to the deep treachery which we had to encounter and defeat.

The first authentic account received at Down from Antrim, was from William Kane, a native of Belfast, who crossed the channel in a boat to Holywood. But the principal leader in that district had fled to a tender that lay in Belfast Lough, for refuge. News went to Bangor, and the people, commanded by James Scott, who afterwards went to New York, secured some guns from a barge that lay in Belfast Lough, and marched to join a body of Killinchy-men, who had defeated a party of the York Fencibles, near Saintfield. They advanced a short distance, when a party of loyalists, mostly belonging to the towns, who had joined through fear, was met, and permitted to return home. They were reinforced by some men from Holywood, and the surrounding country, and learning that a party from Newtownards had received a check at Newtown, they marched in that direction. The soldiers fled on their approach, and left their drums, baggage, and arms with the people. They then marched to Scraby mountain, and next day joined the Killinchy-men at Creevy Rocks, when Munro appeared, and was appointed, by acclamation, to the chief command. He marched direct for Ballinahinch; divided his men into two parties, in order to enter the town at either end, and, on their approach, the enemy fled, and left a baker (the only one in town) hanging at his own door. The main body took post on the hill of Ednavaddy, the next day, about two o'clock, the enemy appeared—horse, foot and artillery, from Belfast. Munro ordered his musketry to intercept them at the Windmill-hill, which they did by a well-directed fire. The enemy retreated, and the people followed them some distance; the troops rallied, brought up their artillery, gained the town, and planted out-posts at no great distance from the people.

A company of young men, called the 'Broomhedge Boys,' from their having sprigs of broom in their hats, dislodged them, with the loss of seventeen of their number, and thirty-six of the enemy killed, and some prisoners, *for the people gave quarter, though the enemy did not.* A troop of the enemy's horse was cut off in the night, by an out-post of the people which was all that happened during the night. Early in the morning, Scott, of Bangor, led a select party into town, under a heavy fire from the enemy stationed in the houses on each side of the street, and grape-shot from the artillery in the street. The guns were taken and re-taken three times. The last charge the enemy made, they fell to a man; but the sound of the bugle for retreat, on the part of the enemy, was mistaken by the people for the signal for another charge, which produced a panic, the people fled in all directions; the retreat from the town caused the panic to extend to the hill, and the whole mass dispersed.

The people's cause was finally lost (at least in that struggle). It now only remained for the enemy to attack the memory of the dead, and the characters of the living, and to slander all who had dared to resist their cruelty. Such as could be neither intimidated nor corrupted, were put to death, or banished; and those, whose fortune it was to escape, could not contradict the false reports, with any chance of safety or success.

At this period, confidence was driven back to the narrow circles of well-tried acquaintance, and every stranger was met with suspicion. The names of the inmates of houses were posted on every door; the situation of such as would not surrender on Cornwallis' proclamation, can only be conceived by those who felt it. What induced so many to risk the danger of refusing the proffered terms, I will not pretend to determine; but mine was this—having joined the Union in the spring-time of its strength, from a conscientious conviction of its principles being right, and having had no reason to change my opinion, when the society was overtaken by adversity, I felt bound to that cause to which I had pledged my life along with my countrymen, and I considered to surrender under the proclamation, was not only a recantation of one's principles, but a tacit acquiescence in the justice of the punishment which had been inflicted on thousands of my unfortunate associates.

To hold up my hands for pardon to those who had imbrued theirs in the blood of my associates, seemed to me to carry with it a participation in the guilt of the blood of my brethren. Thinking a clear conscience of all things most necessary, and

79

looking to the *Most High* alone for protection, I could not join in any written or verbal acknowledgment of guilt, or solicitation for pardon to any human being. I resolved never to be taken alive; I knew no danger, but that of wilfully and knowingly doing wrong.

They in Ulster, that acted otherwise, gave our enemies an opportunity of shaking the confidence of our countrymen in the other provinces, by constantly reminding them how the Dissenters of the north began the business, and in the time of need were the first to abandon it. The taunt only served for a time to keep up a desire in the northerns to show that the cause in the north had not been abandoned by them. There was an earnest watching of the fortunes of the Continental war at this time. The Liberals, or moderate aristocrats, in some instances, affecting to sympathize with the people, became the channel of intelligence to the enemy, of the hopes and expectations that still lingered in the people's mind. In many instances information of this kind was conveyed without intending perfidy; its being given, arose from the intercourse of the parties with the higher classes. The feelings of the people thus ascertained, kept the government in perpetual apprehension; but their hired spies often raised the apprehension to very unnecessary alarm, fabricating conspiracies, plots, etc.

In this way they fabricated a plot, which they pretended to discover, after the suppression of the rebellion, amongst the state prisoners in Kilmainham gaol. The report occasioned a search to be made, when some papers were taken from a man named Ivers, of Carlow, one of the state prisoners, who immediately after was removed to Fort George in Scotland.

The few who were neither to be intimidated nor corrupted, were thus sacrificed in one way or the other, either put to death or banished, or pursued, and forced to fly to foreign countries.

CHAPTER V

I REMAINED at work nearly four months, after the failure of our last effort in the neighbourhood of Belfast and Ballymena. No positive information appeared to have been sworn against me, and so far, I was fortunate enough to escape the fate of my noble leader, and of many of my brave companions. But still I was a marked man, and was compelled for years to wander from place to place, and avoid my enemies. During this period many circumstances came to my knowledge, connected with our struggle, which made a deep impression on my mind, and some of them ought not to be forgotten.

James Hunter, of Glenely, near Glenarn, was a respectable farmer, and well beloved by every honest man who knew him; when the people assembled in arms, on Balare Hill, above Glenarn, he appeared among them. Squire Boyd, of Ballycastle, came to his house, some days after the dispersion of the people with his yeomen, early in the morning, roused him and his wife and family out of bed, set a ladder to a tree before his door, and fastened a rope about his neck, and setting his house on fire, had him mounted on the ladder ready to turn him off. While the yeomen were about their hangman's work, Boyd inquired, of the unfortunate man, if he had any confession of his guilt to make, or any thing to say. Hunter, who had previously in vain supplicated to be heard, cried out—there is a child in that house, an orphan, who was brought up by me—if I saw it out unhurt, I would be content to die: but the house began to burn with such fury that no one dared to enter. Boyd ordered the yeomen to take the prisoner down and let him venture in. He was taken down, and, the moment he was unbound, he rushed into the house. He knew well that no child was there, he ran to a window that was in the gable of the house, and near it was a hollow, where some apple trees grew, which was so covered with smoke, that the yeomen did not observe his escape until they saw him on a lime hill, at a considerable distance, waving his hand for them to follow, which, from his knowledge of the mountains, they knew it was useless to attempt.

Hunter was taken afterwards and prosecuted by a school-fellow of his own, under the following circumstances—the witness's name was Daniel M'Coy, he had joined the yeomen, and the country people had taken some of the yeomen's families as hostages to Balare Hill. M'Coy's wife was one of the hostages, and lay in, on the hill. Hunter had a tent erected on a convenient place, and set a guard over the tent to prevent any annoyance to her or the women that attended her, which M'Coy alleged was a proof of his being a commander among the rebels. Hunter was condemned on his evidence, and lay under sentence of death, nine days in Carrickfergus Jail. By the interest of Sir Henry Vane Tempest, of Glanarn Castle, George Anson, M'Laverty, of Larne Glen, and some other gentlemen, his sentence was changed to banishment, and he was sent to New Geneva, and from thence to the 11th Regiment in the West Indies, from which he escaped to the United States, and got home to his family. He had not been long at home when he was taken again, and by the same interest that had saved his life before, he got permission to go to Norway. The same gentlemen subsequently got permission for him to return home with his family. He had not been very long at home, when the cattle of his neighbour, the man on whose evidence he had been convicted, were seized on for debt. As soon as Hunter heard of the distress the man had fallen into, he went to him, entered bail for the debt, and relieved the cattle. I happened to be on a visit at Hunter's when the prosecutor came to him for a receipt, in discharge for the debt which had been punctually paid by him. He talked of his having kept his promise, and began to boast of his honourable conduct. Hunter took no notice of his boasting, but I did, and took some pains to show him the difference between Hunter's conduct and his own. I told him he must never think of boasting in the presence of a man who had gained two such great victories, for Hunter must have conquered himself before he was able to conquer his deadly enemy.

During Hunter's exile, his farm which was valuable, had

been heavily mortgaged, he sold out his interest in it, and went with his family to the United States. I heard of their safe arrival at Philadelphia, but never had any further account of him or his family since his arrival there.

* * * *

Joseph Corbally, a tailor, lived near Nawl. He was a well disposed young man, and when Defenderism was introduced into the counties of Meath and Dublin, he was appointed a captain, but a faction sprung up in his neighbourhood, the followers of which began to plunder in the name of Defenders. The Defenders of which he had the command, were under obligation to obey him, *not in any violation of the law*, but in the defence of life and property. In virtue of this obligation, he procured a warrant, arrested some of the robbers, and delivered them up to the civil authorities. The Volunteers had not then been put down, and he used to discipline his men (the Defenders), as if they were Volunteer recruits, on a hill in the neighbourhood. Archibald Hamilton Rowan, and James N. Tandy, happened to pass, from Drogheda to Dublin, by the road, along the side of the hill, in sight of the parade where the men were mustered, and went up to them and gave them their advice to desist, telling them that their appearing in arms would not serve either themselves or the country; and their parades were discontinued. A magistrate, named Graham, having discovered the circumstance, induced two of the robbers, whom Corbally had arrested, to swear against him, as a leader of Defenders, and had him committed to jail; while he lay in Kilmainham for trial, Graham offered him his liberty, and a large reward, if he would swear against Rowan and Tandy.

Corbally, after his trial was over, told the offer he had from Graham, to the gentlemen whom it concerned, who commenced, or talked of commencing, a suit against Graham for conspiring against their lives. Corbally had no witness but the jailer, and he swore that he was drunk at the time, and could not remember the conversation, and Corbally was sentenced to four years transportation to Botany Bay. On his way to his destination, one of the convicts told the captain of the vessel that there was a conspiracy to murder him and the crew, and turn pirates; he pointed out as leader, whose name I have forgotten, and Corbally being observed as the acquaintance of the man that was accused, was put in irons along with him. The man was tried, and condemned, and flogged to death, and Corbally lay for three days handcuffed to his corpse, before it was committed to the sea. Before they landed, it was found out that the information was false, and the captain flogged the informer severely. When his term of banishment had expired, Corbally returned to England in a South Sea whaler, came to his own country, and died with his widowed mother at home.

At the beginning of the short peace, the Orangemen of Dublin held their usual rejoicings on the 12th of July. Cavan-street was then the residence of many of them, mostly nailors. An opposite party, in the neighbourhood, took a notion, that being then at peace with France, they might lawfully hold a day of rejoicing on the 14th, which they did by dressing the fountain, in Cavan-street, with green boughs. The Orange party, who were mostly yeomen stood inside of their doors with loaded arms. A tall young man, named Ryan, a wine-porter, passing through the street, being a Catholic, but not at all concerned in the business, was shot dead by a nailor named Shiels. The nailor was sought for, and proclaimed by the magistrates, but was concealed in the Royal Barracks. This was disclosed by a soldier from the barrack to a friend of mine; but who dared to go there to apprehend him? I had no knowledge of any of the relations of the deceased; but I had some knowledge of Counsellor M'Nally, so I went and told him, that if he would procure me a warrant, I would go to the barracks, present myself to the commanding officer, and point out the very room in which the murderer was. M'Nally seemed highly pleased, and desire me to call in the evening, and he would have the warrant, which I did. He then put me off until next morning, when he sent his son with me to Justice Greenshields, of Bride-street, with whom he stayed in private for about ten minutes; and then, coming out of the office with the justice, he said to him (pointing to me), this is the man. The justice then asked me my name, and where I lived, my business, and if I was any relation of the deceased; and, being answered no, he asked what interest I had in pursuing Shiels. I said none, but the common interest, that people might feel, who wished, to be able to come and go through the streets, about their business, without being shot; but if his honour did not think proper to intrust me with the warrant, I had no right to insist; and telling him where Shiels was to be found, I walked away. While I was doing this, word arrived that Shiels was gone off with a party of soldiers. A number of the Liberty-boys set off to keep them in view, if possible. They met the soldiers returning without Shiels, and, being then convinced of his flight, two of the party, one Donally, who had served with Shiels, in the Tipperary Militia, and a lad named Barry, continued the pursuit.

An uncle of the deceased was called on, and acquainted with the step I had taken; he applied to Greenshields for a warrant, and it was granted to him. The uncle, accompanied by Edward Finn and myself, then began our pursuit.

Shiels had left the barracks in the morning, and the same day, at sunset, we were at Castleknock, on the track of the murderer. We passed through Dunshaughlin at dusk; we observed Donally standing at a door. He had overtaken Shiels, who said he meant to travel by Enniskillen for Derry; but, a car-man joining them on the road, Shiels agreed for a seat on his car into Navan, and Donally, having no money, was forced to return. At day-break we set out, and passed through the town of Kells, where Shiels had told Donally he expected to meet friends, and stop, perhaps, two days. Barry was left at Navan, on the look-out; others were left on the watch at Kells, and the uncle and I continued our journey in another direction.

The uncle, an old soldier, who had the ague, in the West Indies, was unable to continue the chase, so I proceeded, alone, as far as Butler's-bridge, where I had some acquaintance closing that pass also; but, on my return, I learned that Barry had arrived, and had met with Shiels in a public-house in Navan, and being asked by him, or some of his company, to drink a toast which he did not like, Barry went out, seemingly in a huff, and returned with a constable, and arrested him, and had him confined; but the magistrate, having no information to warrant his committal, could only detain him for twenty-four hours. He, therefore, sent Barry forward with a carriage in quest of his uncle, who had the warrant, and thus, our object having been accomplished, I set out for Dublin. Shiels was committed to goal in Navan, and from thence transmitted to Dublin.

When his trial came on, Counsellor M'Nally called the strongest evidence, which was so clear, that no jury could have acquitted him; but it was so contrived that the jury sat out the commission, and were discharged. A day was appointed for a second trial, he was again brought before a jury. The judge, in charging the jury, said—'gentlemen of the jury, I see this is party business.' And so the murderer Shiels, was acquitted, and rewarded by government, by being appointed to the situation of a guard of the mail coach; what became of him afterwards I know not, but Ryan was not his first victim.

Of my many escapes from danger, there was one which I had great reason to be thankful for. I had been working at my trade in Dublin, from the time I came from Tullamore. The house where I lived was next to one in which a tailor, named Oder, lived, who belonged to Major Sirr's gang. He was what we called a guinea-pig, from the wages which he received weekly, for attending every night, at Smyth's in Crampton-court, off Dame-street, with such information as he could procure. In the house where my family was, there was a very honest man, named Edward Holmes, who was very kind to my wife and children; he was a slater, and, in the course of his business, he fell into a job in which the notorious Hugh Woolahan was also employed. Holmes being a United-man, and an unsuspecting one, was also persuaded by Woolahan that he was a friend also. Holmes invited him to dine at his house, and, while at dinner, told him what a fine fellow lodged up stairs, to whom he would introduce him the first opportunity. When I came home at night, he told me that a friend of our cause had dined with him, from Wicklow or Wexford; and, on hearing his name, 'take care,' said I, 'it is not Woolahan the murderer you have, for whose acquittal the officers who sat on his court-martial were censured by Lord Cornwallis.' Holmes met him going to work next morning, and asked plainly if he was that man, he denied it, and said he was only his brother; but as soon as Holmes went to work, he was warned, by stones and brickbats falling near him, that he was not among friends, and he was glad to get his ladders and his life safe out of it. Shortly after, the wife of Oder, the tailor above mentioned, called on my landlord, John Golding, and said she had a secret to tell him, if she durst, that might be useful to some of his friends who were in danger; but he kept his distance, alleging, he knew of none of his friends being in danger at all.

One evening, shortly after this occurrence, I had to go to Cork-street, and did not go straight home, which was fortunate for me, for when I came home, a man at the door told me that men of a suspicious appearance had been inquiring for me, and that one, who called himself Adair, a carpenter, said I had appointed to meet him that evening; that there were several of them, and that they parted three and three, and went different roads. My own son James, then about seven years of age, came up, and said, that bad-looking men were there, he saw their pistols under their coats; I then ran upstairs, but Rosy had been invited to spend that evening at Mr Palmer's. I went downstairs immediately, and Mrs Barry, whose husband had given me the first warning, met me, and showed me three of the gang at the corner of Little Longford-street. I observed a boy under a lamp opposite, in the lane; I left the house and walked smartly down the lane, with a pistol cocked in each hand, expecting to meet some of the party, and, on turning the corner, I observed the boy following me, whom I had seen under the lamp: I went down Great George's-street into Dame-street, and over Essex-bridge to Chapel-street, to warn a man named Kirkwood, with whom I had been that evening, that he might be prepared if the search came.

The boy who had followed me all this way passed me as I entered Bolton-street, and ran before me, I at first thought that Coffey's house might be guarded, and that he was going to warn the guard of my approach, but observing him stop at a gateway, and place himself close up to the gate, I sprang round the corner into King-street, and then turning down by the front of Newgate, and crossing to Church-street by the lower end of Newgate, went up Church-street, and round by King-street, and into the house of one Patrick Martin, a cooper, where I stopped for the night, and next morning sent to inquire for my family, and learned that I had been only gone from home a short time when the guard returned, they stopped there until Rosy came home, accompanied by Mr Palmer's son, William, a very undaunted youth, but of a mild appearance. She passed in through the guard, and they inquired of her if Mrs Moylan was in (the name she went by), she said she was going up to see, and bid Mr Palmer come up—her seeming unconcern deceived them, and she going into the room, next to her own, and biding Mr Palmer goodnight, he was not stopped at the door. Two of our children being asleep in that room, and the third in care of the mistress of the house, Rosy threw off her cloak, took the child on her knee, and sat on the foot of a bed, in a few minutes the guard came up, and, my door being locked, they went into the room where Rosy was, in which there were two men and two women in bed, whom they examined very strictly, but they all speaking with *up-country* tongue, they never seemed to see Rosy at all, and the mistress of the place not being in bed, kept them in talk until they went out on the lobby, and began to talk of searching my room, when Rosy slipped the key to the mistress, and she told them, the woman left it with her when she went out, they then went in, and searched the room narrowly, not forgetting the chimney, but no discovery. Rosy was represented as a woman whose husband was at sea, but as she had not heard of him for some time he was thought to be dead, but some of my clothes being in the room they remarked she must be a curious widow who had men's trowsers in her room, which the mistress dexterously answered by saying that she was well handed, and mended or made for men or women for the support of her children. They then went away, saying they would call and see their widow again. They took a letter which we had been both writing, which they noticed, but no clue was in it for them. As soon as they were gone, and the hall-door shut, Rosy took her bed, and the children, down to Mr Holme's room, for the night, and, at the first light in the morning, the informers returned, and were told she had left the house on hearing of their visit, and no one knew, or wished to know, where she went. Oder, the informer, lost his berth, he was taken and sworn to as a deserter, and sent to a condemned regiment.

When I arrived in Dublin, in 1798, it was then believed, by the best informed of my friends, that Lord Edward's arrest was occasioned by the imprudence of a girl in Murphy's house, in Thomas-street. But at a much later period, in 1815, I was informed by the wife of an employer of mine, John Blair, who had been a soldier in the Antrim Militia, that she was in the Royal Barracks, Dublin, the day that Lord Edward was taken; and that it was known to the soldiers' wives, the whole afternoon of that day, that Lord Edward was in the house of Murphy's, the feather merchant in Thomas-street; she said, that one of the soldier's wives had been employed to wash down Murphy's stairs, that Lord Edward had been downstairs when she began to work, and had sprung lightly past her, leaving the marks of his shoes on the newly washed stairs, and when he was out of hearing she cursed his feet, but the servant girl, who heard her, said, 'why do you speak so rude to a gentleman—'. 'He is some scut,' was the answer. 'Oh,' said the girl, 'that is Lord Edward Fitzgerald.' This agreed so well with what I had heard in Dublin, that I thought it likely to have gone from the barracks to the castle. Nor did I hear any other reason given for the discovery, although I had recourse to Dublin for eight years, immediately after the transaction, and had access to men of all ranks, that had been kindly to our cause.

CHAPTER VI

AFTER THE BATTLE OF ANTRIM, I remained in the north, till the month of November, 1798, when I was compelled to quit that part of the country to avoid being arrested. I proceeded to Dublin, where I was joined by my wife and child, in the summer of 1799, and worked there at cotton weaving, until I was employed by Mr Charles H. Teeling, who was then establishing a bleach green at the Nawl, in the County Meath.

While I was living at Mr Teeling's, a poor fellow who had been discharged from the Armagh militia, and was returning home with his family, his wife and children fell sick on the road near Mr Teeling's, and got a lodging in a farmer's barn for a night, but learning it was fever, they were turned out next morning; being unable to travel farther they lay down in a ditch on the roadside. I found them in that miserable situation, and told Mr Teeling of it, he sent his men that instant, and before night had a booth erected and thatched, fit to resist the heaviest rain, and had the family provided regularly with plenty of clean dry wheat straw; by his assistance and support the family were all restored to health, and enabled to pursue their journey. I worked at weaving with Edward Finn, in the Liberty, till June, 1799. Circumstances then obliged me to move my quarters. I went down to Mr Charles Teeling's place, at the Nawl, in the County Meath, and remained in his employment, as over-seer of his bleach green, till 1802. A foreman of Mr Teeling's, named John M'Carroll, give information against me. I then had to fly, and return to Dublin. With the assistance of Mr Teeling I set up a small haberdasher's store, at No. 8, on the Coombe, and I remained there till the month of June, 1803. I had formerly worked, for a short time, with Mr

Lawrence Tighe, in his bleach green at Blue Bells, near Dublin. Tighe one day asked me a question which caused me to think he was an informer, and I immediately left his employment.

The place I lived in, on the Coombe, was directly opposite a temporary barrack, where a company of soldiers was stationed. In the spring of 1803, James M'Gucken, the attorney of Belfast, called upon me for information, which I refused to give him. I had a comrade, a native of Dublin, who had settled with his family in Belfast. Russell had sent for him, and this he had told to M'Gucken. The latter followed him to Dublin, accompanied by Cornelius Brannan, a tailor, and called on me, at my little place on the Coombe, to inquire for my comrade, and to put other questions to me which I did not answer. He then offered me money to quit my connection with the United Irishmen. 'If you have fulfilled your obligation to their society,' said I, 'you can quit when you choose; but it does not seem to me that I have fulfilled mine yet.' 'Well,' said he, raising his voice, and speaking angrily, 'tell your comrade to see me before he leaves Dublin, or by—I will be his death.' I had a case of pistols lying in the desk behind the counter loaded. I took them out, and levelling one of them at him, and pointing with the other to the barrack, I said, 'James, I know the guard is there, you have shewn what you are, I will shew you how little I regard your threat.' 'Ah, Jemie,' said he, recovering himself, quickly, and forcing himself to smile, 'I never thought it would come to this, between you and me.' 'It is your own doing,' said I. He asked if we could not have some thing to drink, in order to shew that we were friends again. I replied that I was not his enemy, unless he forced me to be such. I sent out for some porter, we drank out of the same vessel, and the unpleasant affair went off as a joke. My landlord lived next door. The moment M'Gucken left my shop, I went to the former, paid my rent, packed up my little property, and that evening I quitted the house. M'Gucken came next day, at ten o'clock, accompanied by an officer of the Liberty yeomen, and a gentleman whom my landlord did not know; but the bird had flown.

A few days before, I received a note, stating, that if I would walk, on a certain evening, between Roper's Rest and Harold's Cross, I would meet a friend there. I went, and found Robert Emmet waiting for me.

From the Coombe, I removed, along with my wife and an infant, to Butterfield-lane, near Rathfarnham, to a house which had been taken by Mr Robert Emmet. During my residence there, I assisted Mr Robert Emmet in all his operations, until Mr Russell required me to go with him to the North.

I first became acquainted with Russell, in Belfast, soon after the United system came into operation. He honoured me with his friendship—friendship, which, ripening to the utmost extent of human confidence, continued during his life, and will continue to endear his memory during mine.

It was previous to my meeting with Mr Emmet, that Mr Neilson, at the risk of his life, returned, without the permission of government, from banishment, and that he applied to me to accompany him to the North. This was in 1802, when I brought him there, and back again, to Dublin, in safety.

It was in 1803 that I was sent by Mr Emmet to the North, with Mr Russell. On our failure there, I went with William H. Hamilton, the brother-in-law of Mr Russell, to Ballyboy, in the County Monaghan. I kept him there, in safety, at Mr Crawford's, for a long time. He left that place, against my will, and was taken in a cabin, in the neighbourhood, and I, having been seen in his company, that part of the country was no longer safe for me.

I went to Drogheda, and fell to work, where I remained, until the 12th of July, 1804. I found my wife, after all the perils she had escaped, the same in cheerfulness, in hope, in patience, in fortitude, I had ever found her. She had gone through scenes, which tried some of those qualities.

In 1803, a short time after Henry Howley's arrest, and the death of Hanlon, who was shot by him, while the soldiers were bringing Hanlon's body on a door, through a street in the Liberty, my wife was passing, with her youngest child in her arms, having under her cloak, a blunderbuss and a case of pistols, which she was taking to the house of Denis Lambert Redmond, who suffered afterwards. She stepped into a shop, and when the crowd had passed, she went on, and executed her orders. On another occasion, she was sent to a house in the Liberty, where a quantity of ball-cartridges had been lodged, to carry them away, to prevent ruin being brought on the house and its inhabitants. She went to the house, put them in a pillow-case, and emptied the contents into the canal, at that part of it which supplies the basin.

After having visited my family, I quitted Dublin, and settled down to work, at Rathar road, from Tullamore to Tyrrell's-pass, in the County Westmeath, where I continued, until I received news of my wife's illness, who had been worn out, by

91

attending our youngest child, (who was ill of the small-pox). We had then three children in Dublin, and one in the North. I worked in this place, about a year and a half, at my trade, and paid, with my earnings, the debt of a poor family, amounting to thirteen pounds. I returned to Dublin, and when the child recovered, I fell to work, at corduroy making, until compelled, by the vigilance of my pursuers, to fly once more, when I proceeded to the vicinity of Ratheath, in the County Meath, and remained there, till the times began to be settled.

From the period of the failure of this last effort, nothing remained for me, but to baffle the designs of the enemy against myself. I went about armed, for three years, determined never to be taken alive, avoiding all connection (with a few exceptions) with men above my own rank, still working for my bread, or on a journey, in search of work, or to see my family, who were then in Dublin. I went with a brace of loaded pistols in my breast, but I never discharged them, during all that time, at any human creature, although I had repeated opportunities, to have cut off Major Sirr, and many other enemies, singly, with the greatest safety to myself. I never felt myself justified in shedding blood, except in cases of attack, which it was my good fortune to evade.

In the summer of 1805, I stopped for a few weeks, and wrought with a farmer in the country, who took me aside one day, and said, 'Do you know my landlord?' 'Who is he?' said I. 'He is the Marquis of L——,' said he, 'and is one of ourselves, and wishes to see you, and I think he would give you some money, to help you, and your family to America.' 'I do not know him,' said I, 'and cannot conceive how he knows me.' 'He was with Mr Emmet, when Russell and you parted with him to go to the North,' said he, (I had seen two gentlemen, at Mr Emmet's, in Butterfield-lane, whom I was informed, were, the then Lord W——, and the other, Mr Fitzgerald, the brother of the Knight of Glyn); and he said, 'he is afraid you will be taken.' 'You may tell him,' I replied, 'I will never be taken alive. Thank him for me, for his humane offer; but if I were inclined to prosecute him, I could not identify him, having only seen him by candle-light, and cannot remember one word that ever I heard him say. You may tell him, I will never have any connection with any man, of his rank, and would not give up the protection I have, for the king's. I am in charge of a higher power than that of man.'

At the death of Pitt, the system underwent a change. The

Castle spies were discharged, and the state prisoners set at liberty. My wife sent in a memorial to the Duke of Bedford, in her own name, acknowledging that I had fought on the side of the people, and had been driven, like thousands of others, unwillingly, to do so. She was given to understand, I would be permitted to take my chance with the civil laws, and an assurance was given to her, by the secretary, that no information, on oath, had been laid against me, at the Castle, but merely insinuations against me, and suspicions had been communicated, by the gentlemen in Belfast.

Fleming, one of the witnesses against Robert Emmet, by whom I had sent arms and ammunition, into the Depot, in Thomas-street, much as he had been questioned, and tampered with, had never mentioned my name, either on the trial, or in his sworn informations.

I resolved to return home, and brave my secret enemies to their face, to call on them for employment, or their interest to procure it. Many made fair promises, which (like their former oaths) they never fulfilled. I was, at length, employed by Mr William Tucker, an Englishman, who, although a true friend to human liberty, had never been concerned in any of our associations. I served him for nine years, the latter five of which was at his factory, at Glenford, near Larne; and, on leaving his employment, I returned to Belfast, where I now remain.

Could I have kept a journal, with dates, materials would not have been wanting, for a narrative of some value; but that, being impossible, I have only given detached recollections, as they occurred to me, at various times, of the most remarkable of the events, in which I was an humble actor.

The power that has, through life, preserved me, is doing the work, to which my poor efforts were directed. It is further in advance, than I expected to live to see it. It is past the power of human resistance to prostrate it. Its progress is employing every intelligent Irish mind. Every step throws fresh light on the subject, that engages it, whether of success or defeat. The mind of the nation lives and grows in vigour. Its object is still before it; and as one of its promoters sinks into the grave, another is still forthcoming. Even self-interest, that was so strong against the nation's interest, is coming round to the latter. Hope for success, under all circumstances—have your heart. You may live to see Ireland what she ought to be; but, whether or not, let us die in this faith.

CHAPTER VII

THE RESULT OF A long life's experience, and observation of the evils which press upon the people of this land, and render their condition a mournful spectacle to humanity, a scandal and reproach to civilization, and an eternal disgrace to their rulers; and the gist of the opinions I have expressed in the preceding statements, are embodied in the thoughts I have attempted to give expression to in the following observations.

A monopolizing commerce at home, and extensive plunder abroad, furnished our rulers, in former times, with unbounded means of demoralizing the landed aristocracy of this country by corruption, and of keeping down the people by physical force; the result is before us in the misery and wretchedness we now witness, which some foresaw, and sacrificed everything in this life rather than see such dreadful evils entailed on their country. Those evils are now at the bottom of the question, called *the Landlord and Tenant Question*. In the treatment of it, however, matters are left out of sight, which ought to be of primary importance. Who is the original lord of the soil, and to whom was the first grant given—Sacred Scripture tells us, that the earth is the Creator's, and that he hath given it to the sons of men; by what authority, then, can any earthly creatures cut off the intail?

My opinion is, that every such attempt is rebellion against the law of the Most High; and in this opinion I am confirmed by the cause of war, which is the consequence of this lust of the possession of land. No man can have a right to the property of another, which property has been conferred on him by that Lord of the land, who is the Lord of all created things and beings. The true interest of every man, is to protect the life and property of his neighbour, as he would his own, and to cause every man to do his duty, in this respect to society.

The relation in which the tenant now stands to the landlord, is the relation in which the unprotected traveller stands to the highway-man, who holds a blunderbuss to his breast, while he demands his purse.

When we see the offspring of the landlords of one age, the beggars of another, it proves the unnatural relation in which they stood to the rights of their fellow-men, and the ruinous consequence of the violation of nature's laws. It is beyond the power of labour to meet the claims that are made upon it, the thing cannot go on, it must end.

The class which now fattens on taxation, is driven, by pressure of circumstances, to a sliding-scale, with the view of meeting the varying evils arising from famine and commercial difficulties. The time is coming when the sliding interests of commerce, no longer supported on a sound basis, must sink; and the interests of trade must be founded on the true principles of barter, namely, of value for value, and these interests will then serve as a plank to the drowning prosperity of the nation, and to the people, who are daily swept from the soil by the torrent of taxation, and the united claims of landlords, churchlords, and standing armies, for the protection of both.

The soil, which is the social capital, being ever solvent, possession once secured to the cultivator, in right of the labour he expends upon it, and the improvements on it that have been derived from his labour, remuneration will then be forthcoming for him, and the advantages of prosperous agriculture will extend to every other branch of industry. An honest livelihood will then be within the reach of every industrious man of an adult age, Leaving sufficient for all who may be old and helpless.

If one man could labour the soil of Ireland, he might be acknowledged its lord and its proprietor, in right of cultivation, which is a just claim to possession. When we repudiate that claim, we involve ourselves in a war of classes, for a control over the lives, liberties, and properties of each other, by means of force in the field, or stratagem in social intercourse. To establish the cultivator's claim, and ascertain the relative value of labour to its product, is essential to the peace and happiness of mankind. his consummation of social happiness is fast approaching; it is advancing with the rapidity of the decline of aristocratic power, and the wealth on which its existence depends. The landlord and tenant question demands the attention of every Irishman.

There are three heavy burdens, which the law-makers of former ages, have bound on the backs of the people—the landed, the mercantile, and the clerical interests. These compose the oppressions out of which grow the distractions of society, out of which the lawyers and the sword-law gentry live. These burdens having increased beyond the power of the masses to bear, a fixity of tenure is offered to them, to induce them to renounce the title which they have from the Most High, to a subsistence from the soil they labour. The present fixity of tenure is maintained at the point of the bayonet. Let moral force beware of contributing to sustain any, except its just pretensions.

The leading politicians of our day are only balancing conflicting interests; and, whether for want of knowledge, or want of will, they have never arrived at a rational view of the one general interest. They have not thought of keeping particular interests in proper bounds, or preventing any combination of partial interests from invading that which is general.

The soil is not like the objects of commerce, which are only possessed for the purpose of barter; it is the social capital, from the cultivation of which all earthly wants are supplied—food, raiment, and shelter, being necessary to the body, and education to the mind. Every one employed in agriculture, manufacture, and instruction, is entitled to reward in proportion to his industry; and society must protect the person and property of every individual who does the duty assigned him. He who will not perform his duty, has no right to protection.

The Most High is Lord of the soil; the cultivator is his tenant. The recognition of all other titles, to the exclusion of this first title, has been the cause of an amount of human misery, beyond all calculation.

The old aristocracy having nearly run its race, politicians are now striving to preserve some of its privileges from wreck. A new arrangement is proposed to ward off its total fall; but the fall has been decreed in heaven, and all the men on earth cannot prevent or postpone it, because the progress of Christian truth, which is the perfection of good-will and God-like love, cannot be retarded.

We have been journeying through our own land, like the Israelites in the Wilderness, afraid to look our Canaanite landlords in the face, and longing, too often, for the flesh-pots of the old corruption, to which we were directed never to return. The gift of the land of promise, that will give food to the people, lies before our sons at least. My concurrence shall not be given to the scheme of a delusive fixity of tenure, to enable the landlord to continue to draw the last potato out of the warm ashes of the poor man's fire, and leave his children to beg a cold one from those who can ill afford to give it. Is this a remedy for the miseries of a famishing people?

A fixity of tenure—a fixity forever in famine—for those who till the soil, and do not get sufficient from it for the subsistence of their families. The landlord interest has been promoted at the expense of national and individual prosperity. Its main-tenance has been the cause, not only of domestic plunder, but of foreign aggression all over the globe, by sea and land, in the guilt of which every sane adult is more or less concerned, and liable to his share of retribution, unless he uses all the powers of his mind and body to prevent a recurrence of the evil.

This conviction induced the calumniated men of 1798, to incur the perils of resistance to such wickedness, to encounter persecution, banishment, or even death itself, rather than submit to crawl, under oppression, or to crouch at the feet of indemnified culprits in high places, and participate in the unhallowed gains of rapacious cupidity. This conviction, too, encourages the survivors to persevere in the same pursuit, waiting with patience the providential direction of circumstances for the establishment of 'peace on earth, and good will among men.'

In all our social relations, it is our duty to preserve the interests of every individual, so as to make the good of each contribute to the interests of the people. This is the true science of politics; every deviation from it is replete with mischief to the masses.

In former times, we were fooled with the promises of 'reform, from time to time, as circumstances would permit.' The same idea is now couched in other words—'a place bill, a pension bill, and a responsibility bill,' was the former promise: now it is 'a fixity of tenure.' But the seed of moral force, and of natural rights, that was sown during the American and French revolutions, is springing up; the tares are showing their heads, and as the crop ripens, they will still be distinct; they may stunt the stalks that grow around them, but cannot ultimately mar the crop. Parliaments may decree, but nature will have its course. Patriots may modify their demands, but the people will have their wrongs eventually and entirely redressed. The power of the aristocracy cannot prevent the operation of nature's laws; it cannot, even, find means at the present time, to sustain itself; it is unable to pay its advocates, and hardly able to keep the poor from open rebellion against the rich; it has recourse to a parochial law, with a new name, for every year, to restrain a famished people within the bounds of law: this is the last stage and symptom of its decline. Foreign plunder will not be sufficient for the necessities of the state, nor will domestic industry answer the demands made on it at home.

The absolute necessity of opening new sources of subsistence to the people is now evident; that necessity daily becomes more urgent. It must be pressed on public attention by the people themselves, with a dignity becoming the character of men regenerated by temperance, and the exercise of the virtues of fortitude and forbearance. Not like the merciless landlords, of the past and the present day, turning out on the wide world whole families to perish of hunger and hardship, foodless, friendless, and naked, but putting the means of life and comfort within the reach of the industry of the nation.

Commerce, freed from unnecessary restrictions, and established on sound principles, would furnish, in abundance, all the commodities necessary to a people, and the abolition of usury and withdrawal of encouragement from the concentration of a nation's wealth, in the hands of a few great capitalists, would tend to preserve the true interests of trade, and to prevent the fluctuations which arise from fraud, money-jobbing, and a reckless spirit of commercial gaming, that follows in the train of usury. But no one mind is capable of directing the minute application of these first principles, to commerce, in a way which the subject requires.

When we see the social fabric, which is built on the sandy foundation of lordship, leadership, and imperial delegation, shaken to its base, by a hurricane of conflicting interests, pernicious in their nature and results, it is time to look out for a rock, on which to found a system more substantial, leaving the rubbish of our statute books, as an example of the worthlessness of the materials, to future builders. That rock is, self-government, based on popular delegation, from small communities, not exceeding thirteen members of each district or neighbourhood, of determined limits.

CHAPTER VIII

James Hope's Account of the Battle of Antrim

FROM THE TIME that the French appeared at Bantry Bay, the societies greatly increased, but we soon found that what we gained in numbers we lost in worth. Our enemies propagated rumours varying in their tendencies, by which the public mind at one time was raised to the highest pitch of expectation, and at another sunk to the lowest depression. The cruelties practised on the people, sanctioned by the Indemnity Act of the Irish Parliament, left life without security, and innocence without protection. This state of things rendered resistance inevitable. In the months of March and April, 1798, the people were in daily expectation of being called to the field by their leaders; an intention as it appeared afterwards, which the leaders had little idea of putting in execution. The adjutant-general of Down, who could neither be intimidated nor corrupted, had been arrested; and the general of Antrim kept back the signal for a general movement, called a meeting of his colonels and resigned; by which means the whole province of Ulster, which expected the signal from Belfast, was completely disorganized.

The influence of Henry Joy M'Cracken, especially with the Defenders, had caused many people to consider him as an eligible person for a command in a force in which it was desirable to combine them with the Presbyterians. The Defenders were directed by a committee, by whom their chief was chosen, who communicated with the United Irish Society by a deputy. The latter had to fly to America, and the duty assigned to him devolved on Henry Joy M'Cracken.

On his appointment, he had an interview with the adjutant-general, and shortly afterwards I was directed to act as aide-de-camp to one of two persons named, when first called on by either of them. I delivered messages from the leaders I have spoken of to several persons, and was pressed to give their names, which I declined to do, telling them they would be forthcoming when wanted.

On the news of a rising in a south reaching Belfast, I went to the adjutant-general, who said he would call the colonels, to give them their orders; and I went home satisfied that such would be the case, and recommended patience to all those I met with. This was on Saturday, and on the Tuesday following I received a message from the general. I went to him; he gave me a guinea, and directed me to go to a camp which he said was at Dunboyne, near Dublin; that he had ordered the colonels to meet him, and that I was to return with all haste with such information as I could learn, of the state of the south.

I met Henry M'Cracken near Belfast, and he stopped me; and on learning my order, he said, 'you must not go, there is no camp at this side of Dublin; there has been some fighting at a place called Clonee, near Dunboyne, but the men have marched for Tara, and are defeated and dispersed. He has concealed the signal, and must be watched: or the hope of a union with the south is lost.' I answered, 'if he is a traitor or a coward he will have me tried for disobeying his orders.' M'Cracken replied, 'I will put you under arrest, and let him try me. Go home, until you hear from or see me.' I obeyed; he went into town, and was attacked by some yeomen in Hercules-street. A woman, named Hamell, came to his assistance with a large knife; the yeomen fled, and he escaped into her house, got out of town that evening, and came over the mountains to meet me that night.

Next day we learned that the colonels met, and that the general had resigned. We had no communication from the other chief of the Union, but Henry, as his deputy, watched the movements of the United colonels, and learned that, on receiving the resignation of their chief, they had dispersed in consequence of a false alarm, and adjourned from Parkgate to Templepatrick. They selected Munro, and a man named John Coulter (a linen merchant), as persons to whom the command was to be offered: the first met with, to be applied to, and the proposal made to him. The colonels were to meet on Sunday at Ballyeaston. They did meet; and Henry and I went to watch their movements, and learned that none of them had seen the gentlemen named for the appointment, and that the colonels had resolved not to fight. I learned afterwards that, of three of the colonels who had written notices sent them by M'Cracken, one went in person, and the other two sent their notices to General Nugent.

These orders were sent by the colonels who commanded the districts of Larne, Broughshane, and Lough-geel to General Nugent, which assisted him in his movements to disconcert M'Cracken's plans. The colonel of Broughshane sent his brother to General Nugent, and appeared himself among the people after the taking of Ballymenagh, and assisted in dispersing a body of men who had joined the Braed men in considerable force, on which the men of Kells and Connor fell back from Antrim, and still retaining their arms, took post in Kells, four miles in advance from Ballymenagh, to Belfast. The manner in which the plot was managed to get the Ballymenagh men to disperse, was this: The committee or council, consisting chiefly of men of the forementioned colonels, gave out that they intended to march for Dublin, through the heart of the County Armagh; they sent home the Braed men and others who had fought in Ballymenagh, for necessaries for the march on Saturday evening. The town-guard of the people then consisted mostly of strangers, who, sending on the Sunday morning to the council for orders, found the members of it had decamped. They immediately got into confusion, threw down their arms, and dispersed.

When our general resigned, Henry Joy M'Cracken sent me with a letter to Dr Dixon, who had been appointed to the command of Down. John Hughes, the then unknown informer, was the man who knew where I would find him. It was early in the morning, and few houses were open. I met William Stewart, a coppersmith, in North-street; he went with me to Hughes; we were admitted, and sent up to a room adjoining that in which Hughes slept; he came out of his room half-dressed, wringing his hands in apparent agitation, and exclaimed, 'It is all over! our leaders have sold us; the packing and removal of the plate of—, is the signal for Nugent to commence hanging and flogging the people. There is but one way to stop their career of treachery, and that is to have them arrested; you have done much for the cause, but no service equal to that of lodging information against them.' I told them that whatever might take place, if this proposal was acted on, I would inform against the person by whom it was carried into effect. Hughes still continuing to express his fear and his determination, if taken, to give full information, I took a pistol from my breast, and pointing it at his breast, said, 'If you were not so near your wife and children, you would never speak these words again.' Stewart, who had sided with Hughes, now joined the latter in applauding my firmness, and both declared they were only trying me. I told them whoever would try the experiment on me again would have no time for explanation. They turned the matter into a laugh, and Hughes bade me go to a house in Church-lane, and Dixon would be there. I went, and waited some hours, but he did not come. I then went back to Hughes, and he sent me over the Long-bridge to Mr Pottinger's; but he was not there. On returning to Hughes, he told me to come into town next day but one, and bring a man and a horse with me; that he had some things that Harry would want, that would require a day for him to provide, and I went home. When I went to town on the day appointed, it was strongly guarded by the military at every entrance; it was easy to get in, but how to get out was another question. When I got to Hughes' in Bridge-street, they were preparing to flog men in High-street. Colonel Barber and some officers were walking in front of the Exchange; we could see them from Hughes' window up-stairs, and Hughes seemed greatly agitated. One of Hughes' clerks came up, and said they were flogging Kelso, and in a little while the servant girl ran into the room in haste, and said that Kelso was taken down, and was telling all that he knew. At this time we could see the military moving in small parties in different directions through the street in seeming haste, and Barber and the officers coming towards Bridge-street. Hughes exclaimed, 'They are coming here; what will become of my poor family?' 'What ails you, Hughes?' said I, 'you need not be so frightened.' 'Oh! look here,' said he, taking me into another room, where he showed me a strong linen ticken bag with better than a stone weight of musket balls and some packages of gunpowder. 'I'll ease you of that,' said I, gathering them up and running down the stairs. The clerk followed me to the hall door, and exclaimed, 'Hope, if Barber sees you, you will be hung at a lamp iron.' I gave him a benediction, and told him he and his master might hide, if they did not dare to walk the street, while the horsemen were jostling me, and laughing as they passed. I went into a shop at the upper corner of Bridge-street, where I had left a sack, and put my bundles into it, and then went up North-street, and got a comrade named Charles Scott; we took the sack to a carman's yard, threw it down, and my comrade watched it at a distance, while I put some old things together—two swords, the colours which we afterwards fought under at Antrim, and a green jacket. Having packed them up into as small a compass as we could, we went forth and joined the Town Yeomen, and passing on with the soldiers, as if under their protection, we began to quicken our step unnoticed by the escort, and soon got out of their sight, and striking off the high road by Shankhill, we got safe to the mountains.

The plan of the Antrim movement formed by Henry Joy M'Cracken was sent by express to the colonels of the County Antrim, each of whom was appointed to command five hundred men. The plan, in substance, was as follows.

The different colonels, at the appointed time, are to attack any military post in their neighbourhood; or leave light parties to prevent communication, and march to Donegore-hill; while he, M'Cracken, with the men from the neighbourhood of Kilead, Templepatrick, Carmony, and Donegore, marched to Antrim to secure, if possible, the governor, deputy governor, and magistrates of the County Antrim who were to meet in Antrim on the 7th of June; and to devise means for raising men to reinforce the army destined to effect a junction with the men in arms in the south. Some of the colonels sent these orders to General Nugent, and we were betrayed at all points. We, however, marched to stop the rebellion of the Orangemen against the King's subjects, and not to promote their objects, as some writers would insinuate.

Men at this time were daily driven from their homes, thousands from their country, some by compulsion, some by a kind of choice that was influenced by fear or famine, to be slaughtered on the Continent, or to fly from danger, and to beg their bread in foreign lands: while many persons, not the most unthinking or unsteady in their principles, seemed to be of opinion that it was a question not easily to be solved, whether resistance or submission would be attended with most injury to human life and happiness—bearing in mind that the gagging bills had left no power to public opinion, no protection in a free press, no arena for a moral conflict with oppression.

Some information appears to have been received of my intended journey to the south, to inquire about the Wexford men; for I learnt afterwards that a yeoman was stationed for three or four days at a place I would have had to pass, with instructions to shoot me. Some of my own party wanted to get rid of me.

It was finally decided, when neither Munro nor Coulter

could be found, that Henry Joy M'Cracken should be appointed to the chief military command. He wrote, on his appointment, to Steele Dixon, by one Duffy. The letter fell into the hands of Duffy's wife, and was burned by her.

The South had been forced into resistance on the 21st of May preceding, but the North had been kept inactive until the beginning of June, by the men appointed to command; whether from prudence, cowardice, or concert with their opponents, is best known to themselves. M'Cracken, who was one of the first founders of the Union, and the only one who was not then in the power of the enemy, drew up and signed the fighting orders for the 7th of June, and sent them to the officers who had been appointed, and were expected to direct the movements of the people, but they declined to act.

He set out at length on his march, with a force of trusty followers, which did not at first exceed one hundred men, but from the starting point, having five miles to march, they were augmented on the road by considerable numbers, who considered themselves more as a forlorn hope, than a force having any well-founded expectation of a successful issue.

Having no organized staff to convey his orders, M'Cracken could only give advice, which at first was received with attention by the people. We marched into Antrim in good order, until our front arrived opposite the Presbyterian meeting-house, when a party of the 22nd Light Dragoons wheeled out of the lane below the church, fired on us, and then retreated. Another party then advanced from the same quarter, but was soon brought down, men and horse. The rest of their force fled to the market-house, and we advanced under a heavy fire from a body of foot, covered from our fire by the castle wall and two field-pieces, by a shot, from one of which, a gun we had brought from Templepatrick, placed on a common car, was dismounted. We then went into the churchyard, and silenced the field-pieces, and relieved our pikemen from the shower of grape-shot which they had stood without flinching. Part of our rear had been imprudently drawn up in a field, on the left of the church, and rendered useless during the action. Another party, which had appeared on our right on the Donegore-road, as we entered the town, was ordered to enter the other side of the town, by the back of the gardens. On approach of this party, the horsemen at the market-house, in danger of being surrounded, and being then galled by our fire, made a charge at full speed up the street, some of the troops having previously fled by Shane Castle-road. The body that charged soon fell by our pikemen. At this time, the party stationed on the west side of the town entered by Bow-lane, but were checked by a destructive fire from the men behind the wall, and a volley from another party posted at a house in the lane by which they entered. They were forced to retreat at the moment that a body of five hundred men from Connor and Kells, who had taken Randelstown on their march to Antrim, came to our assistance, and on entering the town, mistook the flying horsemen for a body of the King's troops making a charge, and the retreat of the Bow-lane party for a complete rout. They became panic-struck, and instantly fled. M'Cracken immediately led a party down through the gardens, to dislodge the enemy from their position behind the wall, in front of the demesne of Lord Massarene. This party, however, seeing the flight of the Connor and Kells men, followed their example; and two of them crossing a pike-handle against M'Cracken's breast, threw him down, when attempting to stop them and their comrades. The Monaghan regiment, with Donegall's cavalry, now made their appearance on the road from Belfast, and took up a position at a little distance from the town, and placed two field-pieces on an eminence, the main body keeping behind the elevated grounds, as if expecting an attack, while a party of the Donegall corps surrounded our men who were stationed in the field, between them and the town, and slaughtered them without mercy. We then formed in the street, and proceeded with our colours flying, to the upper part of the street by which we had entered, and kept our ground there until the troops on the hill began to move; we then marched leisurely down the street, and went out by the back of the gardens, on the right hand side of the road, the enemy throwing some round shot at us, which we did not regard, and none of us fell. We retreated slowly to Donegore hill, where we expected to find a body of men in reserve, commanded by Samuel Orr, the brother of William Orr; but they had dispersed before our arrival. There was nothing more to be hoped or to be done; all went home, with the exception of a very small number, of which I was one. Next morning, the news of Lord O'Neil's death reached us. The account of that event I had from some of the men who had advanced, and taken the guns near the market-house. When our men were approaching by Bow-lane, Lord O'Neil came out of a house beside the market-house, with a pistol in each hand, one of which he fired at a pikeman, and wounded him in the thigh, of which wound the man continued lame during life. The man turned round, and seeing the other pistol levelled at him, used his pike in defence of his life. He declared that Lord O'Neil might have entered the castle-gate without any molestation from him, had he only consulted his safety. I believe this to be true, though I was in the churchyard at the time it happened.

Had Lord O'Neil surrendered, the capture and treatment of Major Jackson and others, who did so, is a proof that he would have got quarter, for such was both the orders to, and inclination of, the people.

The troops under his lordship had intrenched themselves in the houses in Bow-lane, to cover their retreat, if necessary, on Shane's Castle, while a light corps, appointed to meet the assailants, were directed to wear each a red thread round his hatband, by which to know each other.

One of the old volunteers who had served under Lord O'Neil, belonging to the Klage company, named Andrew Lewars, whose son fell at his side in the action in Antrim, seeing his boy quite dead, took his pouch and belt, and putting it on over his own, fell into the ranks, and with the additional ammunition during the action kept up a well-directed and steady fire. He escaped in the retreat, and I met him at Muccamoor ten years afterwards, evincing the same fearless spirit.

Samuel Orr behaved like a coward at Antrim; his flight caused a party headed by M'Cracken, who were proceeding to dislodge a body of yeomen in Lord Massarene's demesne, to take to flight, when M'Cracken endeavoured to restrain them, but was thrown down and the panic became general; he then proceeded to Donegore hill, and did not enter the town again. His party diminished in the mountains from one hundred to twenty-eight; Colonel Clavering sent up a letter by a spy to say he would grant terms to all the people, provided they gave up their arms, and give a reward of 100*l*. a piece for each of the four following: William Orr, Samuel Orr, and his brother John Orr, and Robert Johnstone. M'Cracken was not named. Samuel Orr surrendered, and got home. William Orr, still living, was transported; John Orr escaped to America, from Island Magee, along with Robert Orr, a chandler, who died there.

Henry was already at Donegore hill, when we arrived, but on seeing the Kells men going home and our party dispersing in all directions, he and a few of his followers went farther back into the mountains and joined some Belfast friends in the neighbourhood of Glenerry, but for want of some countrymen to learn the state of affairs, they could not ascertain whether any considerable numbers were brought together; but on hearing that the Kells men still remained in arms, they proceeded to Kells. Early on the tenth, when the Kells men were breaking up in consequence of news from Ballymenagh, that the people who collected had been deserted by their leaders, they likewise dispersed. Henry M'Cracken then went to Slemish, with such as were loath to give up the struggle, and remained there until our number was reduced to twenty-eight; we then left that place and took post on the heights of Little Collin, where we heard the guns at Ballynahinch.

On our march to the battle of Antrim, M'Cracken said, 'if we succeed to-day there will be sufficient praise lavished on us, if we fail we may expect proportionate blame. But whether we succeed or fail, let us try to deserve success.' Henry had no other design in making this attempt, than to try the last effort for effecting a junction with the men in arms in the south, and to gain that point he was quite willing to sacrifice his life.

But the fact is, when persecution and ferocious bigotry were stealing-abroad, had we come to a quiet understanding to join in small communities, for the protection of one another's life and liberty, by verbal agreement without any other obligation or design, many a valuable life would have been saved and perjury avoided.

News having reached us, that the men from the lower part of the country were flocking into Ballymenagh, from the 7th of June—I joined them in a few days, and was ordered by the commandant of the town, to open a communication with the Kells men. The town had been taken on the 7th by the neighbours, and they were receiving reinforcements every hour; the commandant told us he had eleven thousand under his command, a thousand of which number had fire-arms, that he intended to march through the County Armagh into Louth for Dublin, and wished me to accompany the advanced guard, which he intended to be composed of the Kells men, to keep them from running home again. I obeyed his orders, and on the 9th we were ordered to Donegore Hill, but the men mutined on the hill, and returned to Kells in the evening. We got billets and kept pickets on the roads all night. The picket on Ballymenagh-road took a prisoner, who told us, that the people of Ballymenagh had been dispersed by the desertion of their officers; we sent a messenger to that place, and found the account was true. Henry M'Cracken having joined us that morning, and seeing the Kells men dispersing also, advised such as were loth to go home, to go with him to Slemish, and keep a rallying point, or let such as durst go home, have time to hear if they would be safe. We went to Slemish, and found a spring at the south end of the hill, which we opened, and we remained there until Colonel Clavering came to Ballymenagh with four hundred men. He sent a message to us offering pardon, and one hundred guineas each, for four men supposed to be with us. We returned for an answer, that the men at Slemish would not pardon him.

We were then reduced to twenty-eight, and learning next day that a female visitor had reported our numbers and means of refreshment, to Clavering, we left the hill and marched in the direction of Belfast in open day, but stopped at Glenerry for the night, and assembled on a hill called the Little Collin next morning. In the evening we heard the guns at Ballynahinch, and marched in the direction of them; on our way we disarmed a guard at Ballyclare, and frightened their leaders a good deal, but hurt none of them. We crossed the country to Devis mountain, and saw several houses on fire in the County of Down. On learning by a messenger we had sent to Dunmurry, that the people were dispersed at Ballynahinch, we retraced our steps, and took post on the Black Bohell; there we were informed from Belfast, that the Wexford men were on their march for the north. We were then reduced to eight men, including M'Cracken, who sent word to his friends in Belfast, that he intended to meet the Wexford men; for although the people were dispersed by treachery, their spirit remained unbroken, and men were calling to us to learn if there was any hope, for the burning of houses, and scouring of the country still continued. Two ladies at this time arrived from Belfast at the risk of their lives, with word that General Nugent was apprised of our intention. M'Cracken then told us that he could make no further use of our service, and after many words of kindness and of grief, he parted with us, and bid us think no more of following him. While we were looking sorrowfully after him, as he was going away to get some place of shelter for the ladies, it being then late in the evening, he called to me and another man, and said he had one more request to make, that we should endeavour to ascertain what the Wexford men were doing, and return with the intelligence to him as speedily as possible; but before we could return he had heard of their defeat, and then crossing the commons of Carrickfergus for Larne, he was taken, and suffered death in Belfast on the testimony of James Beck and John Minis. Henry Joy M'Cracken was the most discerning and determined man of all our northern leaders, and by his exertion chiefly the union of the societies of the north and south was maintained.

His memory is still fresh in the hearts of those who knew him. Forty winters have passed over it, and the green has not gone from it.

I had an opportunity of knowing many of our leaders, but none of those I was acquainted with resembled each other in their qualities and their principles, in the mildness of their manners, their attachment to their country, their forgetfulness of themselves, their remembrance of the merits of others, their steadiness of purpose, and their fearlessness, as did Henry Joy M'Cracken and Robert Emmet.

Glossary

Castlereagh, Lord (1779–1822)
Born Robert Stewart in Dublin. Originally a supporter of reform, but a ferocious opponent of the United Irishmen and strong advocate of repression. One of the architects of the Act of Union and one of the dominant figures in British politics until his suicide in August 1822.

Emmet, Robert (1778–1803)
Born in Dublin. Expelled from Trinity College for his United Irish sympathies in April 1798. In exile in France, but returned to Ireland in October 1802 to organize a new revolutionary effort. Hanged on 20 September 1803.

Fitzgerald, Lord Edward (1763–1798)
Born in County Kildare, the twelfth child of the Duke of Leinster. British Army officer. Fought in American War of Independence. Member of Irish House of Commons. Became a republican in Paris in 1792 renouncing his title and was cashiered from the army. Joined United Irishmen and appointed military leader. Mortally wounded by Major Sirr while resisting capture in May 1798.

McCracken, Henry Joy (1767–1798)
Born in Belfast. Businessman. One of the founders of the United Irish movement. Imprisoned for fourteen months in 1796–97. Led rebellion in County Antrim. Hanged on 17 July 1798.

Neilson, Samuel (1761–1803)
Born in Ballyroney, County Down. Businessman. One of the founders of the United Irish movement and founder of the *Northern Star*. Imprisoned from September 1796 until February 1798. One of the leaders of the 1798 Rebellion. Arrested while planning an attack on Negate Prison in Dublin and held until 1802. Went into exile and died in the United States the following year.

O'Connor, Arthur (1767–1852)
Born near Bandon in County Cork. A member of the Protestant gentry. Member of the Irish House of Commons from 1790 to

1795. Embraced republicanism and became one of the leaders of the United Irish movement. Founded the revolutionary newspaper, the *Press*. Author of *The State of Ireland* (1798). Imprisoned for six months in 1797, rearrested in February 1798 and held until 1802. Rest of life spent in exile in France. Was appointed a general by Napoleon. Uncle of Feargus O'Connor, the Chartist leader.

Russell, Thomas (1767–1803)
Born at Betsborough in County Cork. British Army officer. Served in India. One of the founders of the United Irish movement. Arrested in 1796 and only released in 1802, the longest-serving United Irish internee. Involved in Emmet's conspiracy. Hanged in October 1803.

Sirr, Henry Charles (1764–1841)
Born in Dublin. Became chief of police (town major) in city in 1796. A key figure in the defeat of the United Irish movement in Dublin in both 1798 and 1803. Retired on full pay in 1826 and retained his rooms in Dublin Castle. Long overdue for a scholarly biography.

Tandy, James Napper (1740–1803)
Born in Dublin. Businessman. Leading figure in the Dublin Volunteer movement and one of the founders of the Dublin United Irishmen. Fled to America in 1793. Arrived in France in 1798 and took part in an abortive French invasion attempt. Died in Bordeaux in 1803.

Tone, Theobald Wolfe (1763–1798)
Born in Dublin. A founder member of the United Irishmen. Left for America in September 1795 to avoid prosecution and from there went on to France. Took part in Bantry Bay expedition in 1796 and in Hardy's expedition in 1798. Committed suicide to avoid being hanged. One of the founding fathers of modern Irish Republicanism.